Love is Worth Fighting for
The Meraki Series

If you enjoyed *Love is Worth Fighting for,* please consider leaving a review on Amazon and Goodreads.

Feel free to connect with Effie Kammenou on social media

Website - www.effiekammenou.com
Twitter - @EffieKammenou
Facebook - www.facebook.com/EffieKammenou/
Instagram - www.instagram.com/effiekammenou_author/
Goodreads - www.goodreads.com/author/show/14204724.Effie_Kammenou
Bookbub - www.bookbub.com/authors/effie-kammenou

Sign up for Effie's newsletter to learn about promotions and events - https://www.subscribepage.com/effiekammenoubooks

For additional recipes follow Effie's food blog
https://cheffieskitchen.wordpress.com

Other books by Effie Kammenou

The Meraki Series:
Love is What You Bake of it
Love by Design

The Gift Saga Trilogy:
Evanthia's Gift
Waiting for Aegina
Chasing Petalouthes

Beyond the Social Maze

Exploring Vida Dutton Scudder's Theological Ethics

Elizabeth L. Hinson-Hasty

t&t clark

NEW YORK • LONDON

T & T Clark International,
Madison Square Park, 15 East 26th Street, New York, NY 10010

T & T Clark International
The Tower Building, 11 York Road, London SE1 7NX

T & T Clark International is a Continuum imprint.

Cover design: Corey Kent

Library of Congress Cataloging-in-Publication Data
Hinson-Hasty, Elizabeth L.
Beyond the social maze : exploring Vida Dutton Scudder's theological ethics /
Elizabeth L. Hinson-Hasty.
p. cm.
Includes bibliographical references and index.
ISBN 0-567-02821-6 (hardcover)—ISBN 0-567-02831-3 (pbk.)
1. Scudder, Vida Dutton, 1861-1954. 2. Social gospel. I. Title.
BT738.H56 2006
261.092—dc22
2005025245

Printed in the United States of America

06 07 08 09 10 10 9 8 7 6 5 4 3 2 1

Contents

Preface

Vida Dutton Scudder's dedication to social reform brings the social gospel to life for me. Scudder was committed to the work of numerous activist organizations. Early on in her career, she served as a leader in the social settlements movement, and she taught her students at Wellesley College to share her social passions. She developed a heightened consciousness of the unfair treatment of the working class and recognized society's reluctance to change, yet she was able to maintain hope that the possibility of a more just and egalitarian reality lay beyond the social maze. It was her custom to write about her experiences and to try to persuade others, particularly members of the Christian communion, to work for much needed social reforms. Scudder worked tirelessly alongside many other women and men for a more cooperative social order where persons would be valued in and for themselves rather than primarily for their contribution to industrial production. Regrettably, Scudder's writings as well as the writings of other social gospel women have too often been neglected. This book is an effort to take Scudder seriously as a social gospel theorist as well as to underscore the need for further investigation of the significant contributions that women made to the social gospel movement.

Scudder's published works have been fairly easy to obtain from archives at Wellesley College, Smith College, and other libraries. However, the careful reader may observe that there are still some gaps in the story told in this book. Unfortunately, many of Scudder's personal papers have been either lost or destroyed, making it difficult at times to see clear transitions in the development of her thought. My intention here is to help preserve Scudder's writings as I interpret them. Therefore, when quoting Scudder and other thinkers of her day, exclusive language for God and other archaic terminology is sometimes used. I hope that this will not be discouraging to contemporary readers. Scudder herself kept pace with social advance, and I feel sure that if she were writing today she would have chosen more inclusive wording.

I have had many conversation partners who share an interest in reclaiming and increasing our knowledge of the thought and work of women social gospelers. I have been in dialogue with some through their published writings, and I am grateful for their work. Others I have known personally. I am especially indebted to Beverly Zink-Sawyer, Associate Professor of Preaching and Worship at Union-PSCE, who shared with me her passion for women of the Progressive Era. Dr. Zink-Sawyer allowed me to read her master's thesis on Vida Dutton Scudder and encouraged me to consider a more detailed study of Scudder's writings. Peg Aldrich, Archivist for the Society of Companions of the Holy Cross, and Wilma Slaight, Archivist at Wellesley College, both went above and beyond the call of duty by taking great care to assist me in research and reading earlier drafts of this manuscript. Mentors and colleagues, Douglas F. Ottati, E. Glenn Hinson, Dawn DeVries, Louis Weeks, and Clyde Crews all read chapters of this work and gave sound and sensitive advice on improvements. Thanks should also be offered to the journal *Perspectives in Religious Studies* for giving me permission to use portions of chapters in this book that will appear in an article entitled "A New Womanhood: Vida Dutton Scudder on Women's Public Role in Advancing the Social Gospel." The editorial staff at T & T Clark has been immensely helpful and paid careful attention to detail in editing the manuscript. I would be terribly remiss if I did not also thank my family for their patience while I finished this book. My husband, Lee Hinson-Hasty, not only tolerated long absences and late night discussions while I did the research, but also developed his own appreciation for Scudder and for the Social Gospel. I am deeply thankful for his companionship and interest.

Elizabeth Hinson-Hasty
July 2005

~1~
Why Vida Dutton Scudder?

Nobel Peace Prize winner Emily Greene Balch captured well the connection between Vida Dutton Scudder's pursuit of social justice and her theological convictions:

> She combined an intense love of the Church and Anglo-Catholic ritual and a personal devoutness more common perhaps in the Middle Ages than today, with a radical concern, theoretical and practical, for a more democratic and Christian order.[1]

Scudder was deeply concerned about the role that Christians should play in alleviating social distress. She considered that she herself was part of a broad coalition of enlightened Protestants who directed the attention of churches toward their moral obligation to mitigate the hardships of the working class. These Social Gospelers hungered for God's vision for a new heaven and a new earth to be realized and to transform a social order that had been forged out of competition. Societal restrictions prevented Scudder from considering a professional career as a priest or seminary professor; nonetheless, a highly developed theological vision inspired her passion for social reform, socialist causes, and commitment to and involvement in the Church.

Historians and theologians have paid too little attention to the theological vision that fueled Scudder's social ethic. Only quite recently have scholars given her a serious look as a Social Gospel theorist of some merit. Gary Dorrien commented that she was "one of the most interesting [Social Gospelers who] did what they could to redeem Walter Rauschenbusch's vision of a good society."[2] More often historians have studied Scudder as an activist, Progressive Reformer, and lay leader in the Anglican Church. This book, however, is the first thoroughgoing investigation of her theological ethics. My intention here is to expand our contemporary understanding of women's contribution to the Social Gospel movement and the theology that energized the movement by exploring the conceptual richness of Scudder's thought.

Vida Dutton Scudder, as a woman and a devout Anglican, brought a distinctive perspective to the Social Gospel project. Her theological perspective differed somewhat from that of Walter Rauschenbusch, the most notable exponent of Social Gospel theology. Like Rauschenbusch, Scudder aimed to rally Christian energies to work toward transforming society in light of a commitment to the kingdom of God. However, unlike Rauschenbusch, who emphasized the teaching of Jesus and the prophets, an explicit Trinitarian emphasis informed Scudder's understanding of the kingdom and her social outlook. Scudder appealed to the symbol of Divine Society as a model for justice and equality in her own context. Her distinctive vision integrated her Anglican theological convictions with an impulse toward practical reform.

A Theological Ethicist and a Social Gospeler

Scudder chartered new territories concerning both theoretical and practical aspects of social reform. At one time in her life she held active memberships in fifty-nine activist organizations.[3] It was her intention to help other religiously and socially minded people to interpret God's active involvement in and support for radical social change. Matters of theological and ethical importance consistently emerged in her published works. My bibliography contains ninety-six titles specifically related to theological ethics; however, social questions pervaded even her commentaries on English poetry and novels.[4] Her practical involvements, like her theoretical writings, reflected and nourished her highly developed theological vision.

Although she received no formal training as a theological ethicist, Scudder consistently aligned herself with organizations that provided challenging forums for reformist discussions. She found ample support from family and colleagues to explore both intellectual and practical pursuits. Scudder's family took great care to nurture religious and social interests within her. She was educated at a time when institutions of higher education for women were contemplating how women could extend their sphere of influence beyond the private domain. She and her colleagues at Wellesley pioneered a new curriculum that aimed to prepare women to impact the social order. Friendships with her beloved Companions at the Society of

Companions of the Holy Cross nurtured her and fostered her love of the Church, its doctrine, and its rituals. All of these affiliations contributed to the evolution of her thought.

Scudder was born in Madura, India, on December 15, 1861, where her parents served as Congregational missionaries. She was given the namesake of her father and christened Julia Davida, later called "Vida" for short. While she was still an infant, David Coit Scudder tragically drowned in a river near their home. Vida returned to the United States with her mother, Harriet Louisa Dutton Scudder, and they took up residence in Auburndale, Massachusetts. Scudder's mother became her primary guardian and caretaker. Over the years, she also became a close friend. Harriet and Vida, however, were never left to fend for themselves. Scudder wrote fondly about the support of her extended family. A large and cheerful circle of aunts, uncles, and cousins from both sides surrounded them. As part of a successful and influential New England family, Scudder received a great deal of encouragement to develop into a strong scholar, teacher, and social reformer. Her Uncle Horace Scudder, onetime editor of *The Atlantic Monthly* and literary advisor for Houghton and Mifflin, offered Vida editorial advice as well as a connection for publishing her books.

Despite the tragedy of her father's death, Scudder by most standards led a rather enchanted childhood, unlike the working-class people who later became her preeminent concern. She, her mother, and her aunt Julia Dutton traveled to Europe when Vida was just seven years old and stayed there until she was nearly ten. European galleries and architecture, especially in Italy, lent her an appreciation for the elegance and beauty of art. Describing those years as nourishing to her small being, she wrote about her introduction to the vastness and diversity of the world at a young age. Scudder said that her European adventure "determined what sort of person I should be. Two influences had pervaded me which were always to control my instincts and in large measure to shape my conduct: devotion to beauty, and awed intuition of the human past."[5] People, to her, were like works of art. They were unique in their own way: beautiful, mysterious, and created by an artist whom no one could fully understand.

Returning to Boston at the age of ten, Vida's mother enrolled her in Miss Sanger's Private School for Girls. The Scudders began attending Trinity Church, the parish of well-known preacher Phillips Brooks. Captivated by Brooks's preaching and his far-reaching influences upon New England, Harriet Scudder decided to abandon her Puritan Congregationalist upbringing and to join Brooks's parish. Scudder recalled that at Trinity Church

Harriet "stayed tranquilly content, satisfying her own needs, and those of many whom she gently guided."[6] Harriet became interested in the writings of Frederick Denison Maurice and began to introduce young Vida to contemporary theological conversations concerning social reform. She placed Vida in Mr. Brooks's care to prepare her for confirmation when she was twelve years old. At this time, Vida already felt somewhat befuddled by religion. She admitted that early on she was "naughtily indisposed to follow a popular cry, cause, or person."[7] It took two years for Mr. Brooks to judge Vida ready to be confirmed as a member of the Anglican Communion.

Scudder graduated from Miss Sanger's Private School for Girls at the age of fifteen. She and her mother again traveled to Europe, touring France and England. They stopped long enough in Cambridge for Vida to hear lectures at the university. The year after they returned to the United States, Vida began studying at the Boston Latin School, Phillips Brooks's alma mater. There she received mediocre report cards. Her grade point average was only 81.29.

In 1880, Harriet Scudder enrolled her daughter in Smith College, which at that time was considered an innovative experiment in higher education for women. Her mother chose Smith over Wellesley because she thought male professors would provide her daughter with sounder instruction. Young Vida had mixed emotions about her mother's decision to send her to Smith. She recognized how "brave and modern" her mother was to depart from tradition by sending her daughter to college, but referred to her own secret desire to challenge even more the social boundaries defined for women. Scudder wrote that her mother "made her decision, so far as I remember, without consulting me; for her daughter never confided to anyone the private fairy tale wherein, disguised as a boy, she crept into Harvard."[8] Smith introduced Vida to friends and fellowship over "beer and skittles,"[9] and she found the school a valuable experience, but she never felt that it challenged her enough.

Upon her graduation from Smith in 1884, Scudder traveled to Europe with her mother and a friend, Clara French. While in England, she attended lectures given by John Ruskin at Oxford University. She described her experience at Oxford as an awakening. Ruskin, an art historian turned social critic, was largely responsible for Scudder's social awakening. Through his lectures, Ruskin introduced Scudder to the social questions that would occupy her thought for the rest of her life. She also became acquainted with a new venture in philanthropy started by graduates of Oxford and Cambridge, the University Settlement movement. Toynbee Hall, the center of that movement, was established in the Whitechapel district of London.

Young men from the universities would take up residence at Toynbee Hall for three months, six months, a year, or even permanently. Their intention was to introduce the benefits and beauty of club life to the poor residents of the surrounding neighborhood. Scudder thought of the University Settlements as suggestive for a way to address difficulties facing poor neighborhoods in America's rapidly expanding urban areas.

After returning to Boston in 1886, she began writing her master's thesis at Smith College. The paper was published as a two-part essay in *The Andover Review* and later incorporated into her book *The Life of the Spirit in the Modern English Poets.* With a good amount of fear and hesitation, she accepted a teaching position in the English Department at Wellesley College in 1887. While teaching at Wellesley, and throughout the rest of her life, Scudder could not limit her thoughts and activities to a single course. Pulled in different directions, she chose not to pursue a doctoral degree because writing, teaching, and social activism stretched thin her time and energies.

Early in her career she sometimes wondered if she had made the right decision to teach, but later she came to view teaching as her greatest accomplishment. Teaching gave her the opportunity to prepare young women to act as leaders in a new world order. Scudder was an innovative and creative professor who made a significant impact on Wellesley's curriculum by instigating discussions that helped make connections between the higher education of women and social concerns.

At that time social settlement organizations were gaining popularity and influence. Settlements provided a forum for Scudder to nurture her students' social awareness as well as to test her own theories. Scudder helped to found the College Settlements Association and started a Settlement House on Rivington Street in New York in 1889, which antedated Hull House in Chicago. For several years, Scudder focused much of her energies on the work of Denison House, a settlement in Boston. Of her settlement experiences, she was especially pleased with the contact between Italians and Americans through the Circolo Italo-Americano at Denison House. She thought that programs at Denison House moved beyond the philanthropic approach of much social work.

Through her involvement with college settlements, Scudder became friends with Jane Addams and Helena Dudley. Settlement work taught her about what she called the "patience of the poor!"[10] Her settlement experience left an indelible impression on her, not only by exposing her to the realities of working-class life, but also by informing her of the hospitality of the people with whom she worked. She reflected:

> Living among those very poor people, my sense of values changed curiously. . . . Their amiability, crowded as they were into those mean tenements! Their extraordinary hospitality! . . . With matter-of-fact readiness, in time of need one more child, a derelict friend out of work, any neighbor in distress, would be added to the cramped quarters.[11]

As she continued to distill her own theories with regard to social reform, she concluded that settlement ventures failed. Settlements had never done enough to address the systemic problems that caused widespread social stratification and the poverty of the working class.

In 1889, she joined the Society of Companions of the Holy Cross, a sisterhood of Episcopal women who banded together to pray for God's intercession on behalf of social concerns. Although not a founding member of the religious order, Scudder was a significant force who guided its line of direction. "Mother Vida," as novices under her spiritual direction called her, encouraged her fellow Companions to explore the links between spirituality, Christian ritual, and social issues. Friendships made between the Companions were strong and enduring. Scudder often welcomed these women to live with her for extended periods of time. Florence Converse, a former student, came to live with Scudder and her mother in 1919. Converse had long been a close friend, comrade, and Companion. The intellectual pursuits and spiritual devotion that she and Scudder held in common forged a strong bond between them. They shared a commitment to a cause: the aim to enable a more cooperative social order to emerge through a mutually beneficial partnership between Christianity and socialism. Scudder's friendships with Converse and other women provided her with what she described as a "central peace, . . . victorious over age and circumstance, independent of time or space."[12]

The same year that Scudder joined the Companions, W. D. P. Bliss lured her as a charter member of his Society of Christian Socialists. She began worshipping with the Church of the Carpenter and joined the Brotherhood of the Carpenter. For the next few years Scudder often contributed to *The Dawn*, the newspaper of the Society of Christian Socialists.

Scudder experienced a period of disillusionment with her academic life in 1900, when Wellesley decided to accept a large sum of money from the Standard Oil Company. Outraged that the college would consider benefiting from tainted funds, Scudder contemplated resigning. Undoubtedly, this episode left her feeling exhausted and somewhat insecure in her choice of a professional career. Thinly disguised as Hilda Lathrop, the protagonist in her first novel, *A Listener in Babel*, Scudder worked through many of the questions that challenged her as a result of her breakdown. Scudder collapsed completely in 1901 and did not fully recover from illness until 1904.

She spent some of those years recuperating in Italy. While in Italy, she focused on cultivating a life of prayer and introduced herself to the devotion of the saints. Her study later culminated in two books: *St. Catherine of Siena as Seen in Her Letters* and *The Disciple of a Saint*. It was her fondness and familiarity with St. Catherine's devotion that in time prompted Scudder to return to active social work in Boston.

After returning to Boston, Scudder again invested her energies in the mission of Denison House and organized an Italian Club, the Circolo Italo-Americano. Club programs appealed to Italian intellectuals and professionals. Her activities at Denison House, however, extended beyond the intellectual set. She continued to work directly with working-class immigrants and allowed the settlement to be used on several occasions as a strike center for unions.

Settlement work had prepared her well to consider new ways of thinking about practical and theoretical aspects of social reform. Out of the settlement movement she hoped for a change in attitude beyond the enlightenment of settlement residents. While at Denison House, she had met many labor leaders and attended a meeting of the Central Labor Union with Helena Dudley. At the time socialist theory had gained the reformers' attention; Scudder directed her attention to reading Karl Marx and other socialist theorists.

The Socialist Party seemed to be the logical forum for her to explore possible ways of reorganizing society. When Scudder joined the Party in 1911, she was well aware that religious people often had difficulties with supporting socialism. However, for her, the Christian faith inspired a commitment to socialism. Many of her writings addressed a religious audience suspicious of socialist ideals. She specifically addressed this issue in perhaps her most significant work, *Socialism and Character*.

In 1912, she and her mother made a permanent move from Boston to Wellesley. She felt that the move drew her "into closer union, both inward and outward, with the college which I served."[13] The move also drew her closer to the community surrounding Wellesley. During that same year Scudder was asked to speak to a meeting of women affected by a textile workers' strike in nearby Lawrence, Massachusetts. Her speech was heavily scrutinized by members of the college community and also by members of the surrounding area. Some feared that Scudder had sided with the Industrial Workers of the World (IWW) and that she was becoming too radical.

Scudder argued that her stand in support of factory workers' efforts to secure a minimum wage by no means aligned her with the most radical wing of the union movement.

World War One diverted the attention of social reformers from national to international affairs. This was no less true for Scudder. Although she chose not to write much about the war, she outlined her initial thoughts toward the conflict in "The Doubting Pacifist." She later regretted writing the article, but never regretted America's decision to enter the war. For Scudder, it was a Christian's duty to defend the rights of the weak, particularly those who had never known peace because of the oppressive conditions in which they lived.

The events that followed the war, specifically problems of implementing an ideal socialist vision in Russia, pushed Scudder to consider more deeply the compatibility of revolutionary socialism with her interest in the Christian contemplative life. Clearly, the war had not solved the social problem. She began to direct her interests more toward the Church and Christian models for communal living rather than toward revolutionary socialism. *The Church and the Hour* showed a change in her tone as with great clarity she articulated how her Christianity informed her commitment to socialism.

As her influence grew among members of the Anglican Communion, she aligned herself with organizations that bridged the gap between middle-class Protestants and the working class. In 1919, she helped to found the Church League for Industrial Democracy (CLID). The organization drew upon "broad middle class support by uniting liberals and socialists who would work for civil liberties and industrial reform without explicitly favoring socialism."[14] A central purpose of CLID was to educate Church members about labor issues and the need for reform.

Scudder's mother died in 1920; following her death Scudder had "great need of silence and solitude."[15] She returned to Italy during her sabbatical year from 1921–22. During that year she published *The Social Teachings of the Christian Year*, a book that most clearly established her pairing of socialism with Christian doctrine. She also engaged in a more detailed study of St. Francis and his followers. After her sabbatical year Scudder took several trips to Italy to continue her research and later published two books: *The Franciscan Adventure* and *Brother John: A Tale of the First Franciscans.*

More rigorous study of St. Francis gave her a stronger appreciation of the kind of freedom that the peaceful renunciation of worldly goods could offer. Some Christian communities even had the potential to provide a model for communal living. Her later writings and practical activities bore the imprint of this discovery. In 1923, she attended the meeting of the Women's International League of Peace and Freedom. She joined the Fellowship of Reconciliation as pacifists began to consider society's real need of drastic reorganization. She became "increasingly convinced that no revolution could bring ultimate salvation unless it proceeded from a Christian conception of man."[16] By the late 1930s Scudder's views concerning war had changed. "Foeman Vassals: A Pacifist Apologia," published in 1941, demonstrated her new commitment to pacifism. This was not a popular position to take with regard to World War Two, but Scudder had come to the conclusion that war was the consequence of a society bent on competition. If she were truly to commit herself to a society that functioned by means of cooperation, she had to take a pacifist stance.

Social questions and their connection to Christian beliefs never left Scudder's mind. As new moral dilemmas faced society, Scudder continued to ask how the Christian Church might confront those issues. Even after her retirement from Wellesley in 1927, Scudder lectured on a regular basis, maintained her membership with the Society of Companions of the Holy Cross, and organized groups to discuss Christian ethics and contemporary social issues. She wrote two autobiographies, *On Journey* and *My Quest for Reality*, and continued to try to motivate Christians to take seriously Jesus' call to love thy neighbor. Episcopalians recognized her as an influential contributor to Christian social thought. She was asked to write the biography *Father Huntington: Founder of the Order of the Holy Cross*, an invitation she held in high regard. In 1942, she received an honorary Doctorate of Divinity from Nashotah House, an Episcopal Seminary in Nashotah, Wisconsin. She died on October 9, 1954, in her Wellesley home. Her body was cremated and interred in Mount Auburn Cemetery, Cambridge, Massachusetts.

"I Am No Theologian"

It may seem a bit peculiar that Scudder never claimed the title of theological ethicist, though her titles related to theological ethics surface as early as 1884 and resurface through the publication of her second autobiography, *My Quest for Reality*, in 1952. Nevertheless, she often introduced her work apologetically. For example, her earliest published book, *The Witness of Denial*, analyzed the agnostic mood in the work of modern English prose writers; although Scudder approached the subject as a "Christian and Catholic,"[17] she apologized for her lack of theological knowledge.[18] *The*

Social Teachings of the Christian Year, a book that analyzed the social message found in the Anglican prayer book, bore a similar disclaimer. These "mysteries," wrote Scudder, were not studied "from the point of view of formal theology."[19] In her second autobiography, she simply stated, "I am no theologian."[20]

The disclaimer that is characteristic of Scudder's work showed her discomfort with theologians who focused on abstract theological concepts. While reflecting on the differences between moral arguments written by theologians and those authored by socialists, Scudder expressed her fear that "the theologians are perused by the privileged alone."[21] H. Francis Perry's article "Workingman's Alienation from the Church" confirmed her suspicions. Chronicling interviews with wage earners and their leaders, Perry concluded: "They honestly believe that theology is a scheme gotten up to turn the poor man's thought away from the present life to some dim, mysterious future world, where all his sufferings here will be made up for, and in this way to prevent his trying to better himself and his class by overthrowing the system of slavery which our present method of business entails."[22]

Believing that a particularly "fertile literature"[23] provided the foundation for the theologian's arguments, Scudder thought it essential to make them relevant to the problems of a world deeply divided over issues of class. Her aim was to explore how Christian doctrine informed everyday life. To do this, theological ideas had to be accessible to a broad readership. Like other social Christians, Scudder sometimes chose more popular means to communicate her message. She was in good company when she worked out theological ideas through characters in her three romance novels. For example, F. D. Maurice in *Eustace Conway; or, The Brother and Sister: "A Novel"* (1834) used Eustace to discuss his understanding of human nature and critique of society. About Scudder's novels, Marilyn Howley Smith observed that they were "especially important because in them, Scudder experienced a freedom in creating fictional characters which allowed her to voice her own questions and work through her spiritual confusion in the guise of her heroes and heroines."[24] Hiding behind Neri, the main character in *The Disciple of a Saint*, Scudder disclosed her real concern: "Questions of dogma did not trouble Neri—rather the great question, the proof of dogma in the resultant life."[25]

In a letter to Rauschenbusch, Scudder explained her objective in writing *Socialism and Character*: "Of course I want in my little way to supplement your big work, in showing the religious basis of socialism, not sentimentally, but in a way consistent with all the most practical, and indeed with the seemingly irreligious, phases of the movement."[26] That is, she understood herself to be clarifying the relationship between Christianity and the socialist movement. She wrote to Rauschenbusch again after she reviewed a chapter of his book *Christianity and the Social Crisis* and commented that she saw their purposes as "identical."

> Your purpose is identical with that of *Socialism and Character*, for I too, of course, was trying to break down the barriers between the socialist world and the religious world, and show each its need of the other, by presenting the affiliations between them.[27]

Scudder's insistence that she was not a professional theologian accorded with a similar reticence among other Social Gospel writers. Paul T. Phillips observed that "formal theology presented an 'image problem' for the Social Gospelers in North America, who wanted to avoid any semblance of separating the movement from the general public."[28] In his preface to *How Much Is Left of the Old Doctrines?* Washington Gladden said that his writings were "not for scholars, but for the people. No claim to special theological or scientific knowledge can be set up by the writer."[29] Rauschenbusch introduced the book that was widely acknowledged as the preeminent statement of Social Gospel theology with these words: "Of my qualifications for this subject I have reason to think modestly, for I am not a doctrinal theologian either by professional training or by personal habits of mind." Moreover, he suggested "that the necessity of approaching systematic theology from the outside may be of real advantage. Theology has often received its most fruitful impulses when secular life and movements have set it new problems."[30]

Scudder hoped to set before the Christians of her time the "fruitful impulses" that Rauschenbusch mentioned. Although she wrote as a laywoman, both professionally trained theologians and laity affirmed her contribution to theological thought. Rauschenbusch sent her a chapter of *Christianizing the Social Order* for her comments before he published the book.[31] He also sent Scudder a copy of *A Theology for the Social Gospel* bearing the inscription "Brother and Comrade."[32] Ministers in the Anglican Communion lovingly called her "Aunt Vida." And more recently, Teresa Corcoran has characterized Scudder: "Her greatest contribution has been to religious social thought."[33] Despite the fact that contemporary scholars have more often looked to her as a social activist rather than a theological ethicist, her writings demonstrate her important contribution to the theological ethics of the Social Gospel movement.

Analyzing the basic theological concepts that fueled Scudder's social vision provides the opportunity to see the advantages of "approaching systematic theology from the outside," to use Rauschenbusch's words. Scudder's theology evolved over her lifetime; it was dynamic and living. She admitted that her own theology was "not systematic."[34] True to her statement, no finely tuned systematic organization can be found in Scudder's work. Indeed, she never really fit together in a single self-consistent whole all the pieces in her portrait of a God who is active in messy and unruly human affairs. Still, it is difficult to miss the persistence, depth, and seriousness of Scudder's theological reflections.

A Growing Appreciation for Her Work

Over the last forty years, historians have gained a steadily wider appreciation for the theologians and practitioners who advanced the Social Gospel. Commentators have differently interpreted Scudder's participation in the movement, depending on how one or another of them has understood the movement as a whole. For example, Henry F. May regarded Social Gospel theologians as "middle-of-the-road" clergy,[35] whom he distinguished from Conservative Social Christians and Radical Social Christians. May looked to Rauschenbusch as the preeminent Social Gospel theologian,[36] pointing out that Rauschenbusch organized his theology around the centrality of the kingdom of God within Jesus' social teachings. May then classified practical reformers, such as Jane Addams and Frances Willard, as nonreligious thinkers.[37]

Pointing to especially Scudder's outspoken advocacy of socialism,[38] May placed her among the radical Christian Socialists. However, he failed to discuss possible links between reforms advocated by the Christian Socialists and their theologies.[39] Scudder's work does not fit comfortably into May's three-part model, and one could compare it with Rauschenbusch on a theoretical level and with Addams and Willard on the basis of her contribution to practical reform. We cannot adequately understand her commitment to socialism, however, apart from her interpretation of the nature of Christianity itself. As a social visionary, Scudder contemplated the important role that Christians could play in enabling radical changes in society. Altering the social structure would bring society more in line with the democratic principles upon which the Christian faith was based. She thought that the capitalistic economic environment in the United States stunted the growth of a more just society. Capitalism prevented Christians from living according to a Christian ethic. A new world order could remedy the diseases of individualism and defiant self-protection that were stunting the spiritual growth of Christians. According to Scudder, a mutually beneficial partnership between socialism and Christianity would create the environment in which the kingdom of God could flourish. In an address she gave to the Society of Christian Socialists in March 1891, she said:

> Socialism would render possible, for the first time for centuries, literal obedience to the commands of the Master; it would enable men to "take no thought for the morrow," for it would remove from them the necessity of constant thought for what they shall eat, what they shall drink, and wherewithal they shall be clothed.[40]

Scudder looked to Christian doctrine to measure the fairness of the principles of equality evident in socialism. Successful socialism would rest only on the strong foundation of the Christian faith.

Robert Handy found May's description of the three branches of social Christianity "vague and problematical."[41] In particular, he sought to correct May's mistake by looking more closely at the theology developing out of the Social Gospel movement.[42] Using Rauschenbusch's work as the prototype of the theological ethics of this era, he identified what scholars now count as the benchmarks of Social Gospel theology: the centrality of the kingdom of God, an interpretation of sin as social, and an emphasis on social salvation as opposed to individual salvation. Unfortunately, however, Handy did little to encourage scholars to look at other figures they might consider as contributors to Social Gospel theology. Mentioning Scudder only in relation to her Social Gospel novels, Handy missed her considerable significance for conversations concerning theological ethics. The Trinitarian basis of her theological ethics, her reference to saints as the models for Christian living, and her dedication to practical social reform—these add greater depth to our understanding of Social Gospel theology, especially when we compare her thought to the benchmarks that Handy identified in Rauschenbusch's work.

More recently, Ronald White and Charles Hopkins and Susan Curtis generously interpreted the breadth of the movement on both practical and theoretical levels. Their broader definitions of the Social Gospel movement included social settlement work, Christian Socialism, involvement in labor movements, and contributions to Social Gospel theology. They made room for the contributions of such recognized practitioners and thinkers as Jane Addams, Ellen Gates Starr, and Vida Scudder, who helped to found social settlements in several major cities, including New York, Boston, Philadelphia, and Chicago. White and Hopkins discussed the noteworthy work done by the Women's Christian Temperance Union under Frances Willard's leadership.[43] Curtis linked advocacy for the Social Gospel movement to Christian support of Socialist groups, labor organizations, and unions. She further commented upon the importance of Social Gospel novels written by figures such as Charles Sheldon and Elisabeth Stuart Phelps.[44] Also among significant thinkers that White and Hopkins and Curtis investigated were those committed to developing theory; among them were Richard Ely and Walter Rauschenbusch.

This broader interpretation of the Social Gospel movement invites a closer examination of the work of Vida Scudder as an ethicist and practitioner. Nevertheless, White, Hopkins, and Curtis did not offer full interpretations of Scudder's work. Curtis mentioned her with reference to social settlement work but provided no critical analysis of her writings.

Teresa Corcoran wrote an intellectual biography about Scudder, but her book did not analyze Scudder's theological ethics in detail. Moreover, Martha Boonin-Vail called Corcoran's biography of Scudder a "flawed treatment of Scudder which focuses on her literary output. Instead of arguing that Scudder was a Social Gospeler, Corcoran depicted Scudder as a Progressive."[45] Corcoran did not analyze the influence of Scudder's theological and spiritual beliefs upon her commitment to social reform.

Boonin-Vail offered another perspective, believing that scholars missed the significance of Scudder's spirituality for her social thought and political radicalism.

> Previous investigations of Scudder's life focused mainly on her political thought and activism and have treated her spirituality as either tangential to her socialism or as an amusing eccentricity. Few have seriously explored the connections between her religious faith and her political work. Those who have explored some of the linkages between her religious and political thought have failed to identify Scudder's spirituality as Anglo-Catholic. Therefore, historians have been somewhat misdirected in their attempts to identify Scudder's place among Gilded Age and Progressive Era reformers.[46]

Boonin-Vail concluded that Scudder's distinctively Anglo-Catholic spirituality separated her from Social Gospelers. "Anglo-Catholicism," she wrote, "was a religious movement; as such it was a movement of criticism for alternatives to the religious status quo."[47]

Bernard Markwell studied Scudder's writings in light of her impact on the social movement within the Anglican Church. Markwell suggested that Scudder moved beyond the optimism of the Social Gospel. Unlike many reformers who felt defeated by the disillusionment they experienced in the face of failed reforms, Markwell thought that Scudder's theology of the cross "recognized and transcended catastrophe and defeat."[48] Despite sometimes disappointing results, Scudder was able to continue her activism until the end of her life because of her theology of the cross.

It is true that an undercurrent of realism is evident in Scudder's theological outlook. She thought of suffering as a theme of vital and irreplaceable importance in the Christian story. A perfect, Utopian paradise would always remain out of society's reach. Her concept of the value of suffering was informed by her understanding of God in terms of the Trinity. Trinitarian doctrine also grounded her optimism about human achievement during the Social Gospel era and the years following World War One. Though she thought the term "Social Gospel" was overused,[49] she never moved beyond the idea that human beings could significantly impact their social environment and restore it to greater harmony with the God who created it.

I agree with Markwell and Boonin-Vail that one must understand Scudder's commitment to the Anglican Church to comprehend fully her ethical positions. I also think that Boonin-Vail was right that a strong grasp on Scudder's spirituality is necessary to understand fully her social and political commitments. However, I do not think that Scudder's Anglo-Catholic spirituality excludes her from being considered among the ranks of Social Gospelers. Rather, I think that the distinctiveness of Scudder's approach will more fully inform our understanding of Social Gospel theology.

Anglicans were among the front-runners of the Social Gospel movement, and scholars have held Scudder to be a prominent contributor to the Episcopalian Social Gospel. She also aligned herself with other reformers commonly associated with the Social Gospel, and she gained a great deal from their insights, particularly from the work of Rauschenbusch. Indeed, she thought of Rauschenbusch not only as a friend and colleague but also as a "comrade" in the struggle for justice for working folks.[50] Social Gospelers, Rauschenbusch among them, emphasized the importance of spirituality and a personal encounter with God experienced through serving the poor. On occasions Rauschenbusch had been outspoken against asceticism, but Scudder teased him about being a social mystic.

My intention here is to build upon the work that scholars have already done on Scudder by surveying her achievements as a significant theological ethicist of the period. Scudder is one of the few female theologians to whom we can look for insights regarding the Social Gospel. I will focus on the conceptual richness of Scudder's theological ethics, identify her contribution to Social Gospel theology and highlight the importance of her enduring legacy. Allowing her social outlook to grow from the fertile ground of her Trinitarian faith, she offered a distinct perspective on Social Gospel theology.

A Systematic Exploration of Scudder's Thought

Vida Dutton Scudder's Trinitarian faith lay at the heart of her theological ethics. She believed that Christian doctrine opened a doorway to a new world in which the Trinity inspired democracy. The Divine Society of three-in-one became the basis for the pursuit of equality and justice in a society that would progress toward the Cooperative Commonwealth. This dynamic relationship between her religious beliefs and social advocacy enabled her to envision a mutually beneficial partnership between Christianity and socialism.

Chapter 2, "Vida Dutton Scudder's Theological Vision," discusses her understanding of the Trinity, Jesus' teachings, and inspiration of the Spirit within the work of the Christian community. Scudder viewed the human journey as an adventure of traversing a spiritual landscape in search of union with the Eternal.[51] The journey involved considering the greater "Reality" beyond the social maze evident on the sensible plane. Drawing upon her knowledge of Christian teachings, Scudder believed in a God active in and discernible through natural and worldly affairs:

> Final Reality that controls the secret thought is no distant Monarch, the natural ruler of a world aristocratically organized, but a pervading Spirit, so manifest in the life of nature and the social whole that it is easy to confuse Him with the very world which He inspires.[52]

God's active involvement in the world revealed the secrets of the kingdom hidden beneath the inequalities of the social maze. Looking to the Gospels for assistance, Scudder interpreted Jesus as a chief social idealist who, by his teaching about the kingdom and willingness to sacrifice himself voluntarily for the sake of others, meant to herald in a reign of justice and social equality. Jesus pointed Christians to something beyond the social maze. According to Scudder, we best understand incarnation as being drawn "Elsewhere," beyond social inequalities and toward the "Absolute" for which Christians long.

However, the ground of Christian social hope was not resident simply in her understanding of Jesus' ministry. Jesus' life and teachings exhibited the procession of the Holy Spirit and the union of God with the natural order. Jesus revealed the work of the Trinity in the temporal process. The Trinity shows God's "daring effort to reveal something of the nature of ultimate reality."[53] The Divine Society symbolized by the Trinity grounds social hope. Indeed, "the Blessed Trinity is to the Christian the prototype of the social order which man, because he is made in the image of God, is bound to realize."[54] The meaning of the Trinity is in fellowship, not in self-seeking, and provides the basis for a civilization based on equality of rank.

A Cooperative Commonwealth would render the incarnational presence of God more apparent. Chapter 3, "Character and the Cooperative Commonwealth," focuses on Scudder's diagnosis of the social ailment, its impact upon the character of individual citizens, and her vision for a new world order. She envisioned a mutually beneficial partnership between Christianity and socialism, in which Christian beliefs would shape character and prepare individuals to be part of a socialist state. The Cooperative Commonwealth would bear the features of the kingdom, but could not be equated with it.[55] It would be society aiming to make Christ's teachings universal. Socialism would lift humanity to a higher spiritual plane by removing material obstacles that hamper spirituality and discernment. Socialism would support a society based upon democratic principles and rid society of a stagnant political environment that stunted the growth of Christians. The Cooperative Commonwealth would not create a new race, but the character of the existing race would be altered as it entered into a new domain unencumbered by materialism.

Chapter 4, on "Scudder's Moral Reasoning, Sources, and Norms," analyzes the key elements that served as base points for her arguments for changes in public policy: her interpretation of the social circumstances calling for drastic moral action; her understanding of human nature; the moral values, norms, and guidelines Christians are invited to enact; and the ultimate loyalty and causes that she served. Much of Scudder's thought hinged on her interpretation of the current social circumstances. Most notably, she assessed the condition of a society crippled by the spread of capitalism and class antagonism, contrasting it to the ideal of a socialist alternative. Throughout her texts she wove insights from the writings and teachings of F. D. Maurice, John Ruskin, Thomas Carlyle, Giuseppe Mazzini, and a number of English literary figures. Visits to Toynbee Hall in London, significant travel abroad, as well as her involvement in the College Settlement Association and in Denison House helped to shape her carefully developed and contextually minded social conscience. Scudder always worked out her understanding of current circumstances against the background of a vision of and commitment to the Cooperative Commonwealth that was informed by her theology. While the Cooperative Commonwealth would not free society from all suffering (physical, mental, or spiritual), it would encourage solidarity with the poor laborer as well as develop an interest in equality, justice, and community.

Though Scudder was well aware that social conditions shaped human beings, she also based her theories on the premise that human beings could change their conditions. In the right environment individuals and communities could move toward a more just society, in which they might foster their consciousness of God and their social conscience.[56] Thinking that patterns evident in the life and teachings of Jesus and St. Francis of Assisi transcend their historical realities, Scudder felt confident that human beings could develop into better moral agents. She associated their lives with the quest for the Cooperative Commonwealth. They embodied equality, self-sacrifice, solidarity, justice, and community.

All of these aspects of Scudder's moral reasoning supported her practical involvement and activities. Scudder remained committed to ecumenism; to the education of the upper, middle, and lower classes about the effects of class antagonism; and to a wide variety of institutions that supported social equality. Through her dedication to institutions and ventures in the service of equality, Scudder looked beyond her own self-interest and sought the fellowship offered by a more cooperative social order.

The concluding chapter, "Scudder's Social Vision: An Enduring Legacy," judges the impact of Scudder's work with reference to her students and the Society of Companions of the Holy Cross; it also assesses her theological ideas against the next generation of liberal Protestant theologians. Reinhold Niebuhr and H. Richard Niebuhr criticized Social Gospelers for their optimism about the ability of human beings to think and act beyond their own selfish interests. Scudder, however, did not fit perfectly with their views of liberalism. Evident in her thought was an undercurrent of realism that challenged some of the later characterizations of Social Gospel views. As a participant in both practical movements for social reform and as a significant theological ethicist addressing the most pressing issue of her day from a woman's perspective, Scudder's work enlarges our understanding of Social Gospel theology. Her writings maintain relevance for contemporary conversations as they increase our historical awareness of the breadth of the Social Gospel movement. The explicitly Trinitarian emphasis of her theology fueled her appetite for social change. For a world focused too closely on increasing its wealth, God was the model for change. A truly egalitarian society would fashion itself in God's cooperative image.

Notes

1. Emily Greene Balch, "Vida Dutton Scudder, 1861–1954," *Wellesley Alumnae Magazine* (January 1955): 89.
2. Gary J. Dorrien, *The Making of American Liberal Theology: Idealism, Realism, and Modernity* 1900–1950 (Louisville: Westminster/John Knox Press, 2003), 128.
3. Ibid., 160.
4. Scudder wrote *Social Ideals in English Letters* "to consider English literature in its social aspect." Vida Dutton Scudder, *Social Ideals in English Letters* (Boston: Houghton, Mifflin, 1898), 1.
5. Vida Dutton Scudder, *On Journey* (New York: Dutton, 1937), 30.
6. Ibid., 39.
7. Ibid., 37.
8. Ibid., 58.
9. Ibid., 71.
10. Ibid., 147.
11. Ibid.
12. Ibid., 219.
13. Ibid., 276.
14. Gordon Greathouse, "Historical Turbulence of Scudder, Spofford Years," *The Witness* 67 (July 1984): 14.
15. Scudder, *On Journey*, 292.
16. Ibid., 306.
17. Vida Dutton Scudder, *The Witness of Denial* (New York: Dutton, 1895), 4.
18. Ibid., 49–50.
19. Vida Dutton Scudder, *Social Teachings of the Christian Year* (New York: Dutton, 1921), vii.
20. Vida Dutton Scudder, *My Quest for Reality* (Wellesley, Mass.: Printed for the author, 1952), 45.
21. Vida Dutton Scudder, *Socialism and Character* (London: Dent, 1912), 124.
22. H. Francis Perry, "The Workingman's Alienation from the Church," *American Journal of Sociology* 4, no. 5 (March 1899): 626.
23. Scudder, *Socialism and Character*, 124.
24. Marilyn Howley Smith, "Vida Scudder and Social Reform: A Theology of Hope" (PhD diss., St. Louis University, 1996), 326.
25. Vida Dutton Scudder, *The Disciple of a Saint: Being the Imaginary Biography of Raniero di Landoccio de Pagliaresi* (New York: Dutton's; London: Dent, 1907), 201.
26. Vida Dutton Scudder to Walter Rauschenbusch, August 8, 1911. Walter Rauschenbusch Papers, American Baptist Historical Society Manuscript Collection, Samuel Colgate Historical Library, Colgate Rochester Theological Seminary, Rochester, NY.
27. Scudder to Rauschenbusch, September 21, 1912. Walter Rauschenbusch Papers, American Baptist Historical Society Manuscript Collection, Samuel Colgate Historical Library, Colgate Rochester Divinity School, Rochester, NY.

28. Paul T. Phillips, *A Kingdom on Earth* (University Park, PA: The Pennsylvania State University Press, 1996), 28.

29. Washington Gladden, *How Much Is Left of the Old Doctrines?* (Boston: Houghton, Mifflin, 1899), iii.

30. Walter Rauschenbusch, *A Theology for the Social Gospel* (1917; repr., Louisville: Westminster/John Knox Press, 1997), from the foreword.

31. Scudder to Rauschenbusch, September 21, 1912.

32. Scudder wrote a note to Rauschenbusch to thank him for the gift: "How late I am in acknowledging the copy of your book with that delightful inscription. I love to be called Brother and Comrade despite the sex discrimination involved. Of course you know that my great desire is to get your feeling and interpretation over into the Anglican Communion. For this very reason I have stressed, you may think unduly, our points of difference with you, in the Review which you will see some day." Scudder to Rauschenbusch, March 27, 1918. Walter Rauschenbusch Papers, American Baptist Historical Society Manuscript Collection, Samuel Colgate Historical Library, Colgate Rochester Divinity School, Rochester, NY.

33. Teresa Corcoran, *Vida Dutton Scudder* (Boston: Twayne, 1982), preface.

34. Scudder to Rauschenbusch, February 27, 1918. Walter Rauschenbusch Papers, American Baptist Historical Society Manuscript Collection, Samuel Colgate Historical Library, Colgate Rochester Divinity School, Rochester, NY.

35. Henry F. May, *Protestant Churches and Industrial America* (New York: Harper & Bros., 1949), 170.

36. See May, *Protestant Churches and Industrial America*, ch. 3; and Robert Handy, *The Social Gospel in America, 1870–1920* (New York: Oxford University Press, 1966).

37. See May, *Protestant Churches and Industrial America*, ch. 4.

38. Ibid., 244.

39. It is worthy of note that May did not intend to analyze the theology undergirding social Christianity. However, avoiding the central place of theology in social Christianity created problems in his understanding of Scudder's work and that of other Protestant social reformers. May discussed Rauschenbusch primarily in relation to his work with churches, although he was involved in numerous organizations that had a profound impact on this movement. He mentioned social settlements in regard to the progressive movement, although settlement workers often chose to reside in these houses for religious reasons. See Mary Kingsbury, "The Social Settlement and Religion," in *Readings in the Development of Social Settlement Work* (ed. Lorene M. Pacey; New York: Association, 1950), 136–42; and Eleanor Stebner, *The Women of Hull House* (New York: State University of New York, 1997).

40. Vida Dutton Scudder, "Socialism and Spiritual Progress—A Speculation." An address delivered before the Society of Christian Socialists, Boston, March 1891, 13.

41. Robert Handy and Sidney Mead, review of *Protestant Churches and Industrial America*, by Henry F. May, *Journal of Religion* 30 (1950): 67–69.

42. Ibid. Also see Handy, *The Social Gospel in America*.

43. See Ronald C. White Jr. and Charles Howard Hopkins, *The Social Gospel: Religion and Reform in Changing America* (Philadelphia: Temple University Press, 1976).

44. See Susan Curtis, *A Consuming Faith: The Social Gospel and Modern American Culture* (Baltimore: John Hopkins University Press, 1991).

45. Martha Clara Boonin-Vail, "New Wine in Old Bottles: Anglo-Catholicism in the United States, 1840–1919" (PhD diss., Yale University, 1993), n. 133. Boonin-Vail was identifying the term "Progressive" with the social and political activism of reformers of the Gilded Age and Progressive Era. She linked the term "Social Gospeler" with those whom Peter Frederick called "intellectual reformers." Frederick thought that reformers such as Rauschenbusch and

Ely illustrate the ineffective work of middle-class reform due in part to their lack of contact with the working class. See Peter J. Frederick, *Knights of the Golden Rule: The Intellectual as Christian Social Reformer in the 1890s* (Lexington: University of Kentucky Press, 1976), xi–xvi.

46. Ibid., 132–33.

47. Ibid., 185.

48. Bernard K. Markwell, *The Anglican Left* (Brooklyn, NY: Carlson, 1991), 194.

49. See Vida Dutton Scudder, "The Social Duty of Catholics," *The American Church Monthly* 27 (May 1930): 335–42.

50. Scudder addressed a letter to Rauschenbusch with this greeting: "My dear Comrade, (May I call you so?)." Scudder to Rauschenbusch, October 9, 1912. Walter Rauschenbusch Papers, American Baptist Historical Society Manuscript Collection, Samuel Colgate Historical Library, Colgate Rochester Divinity School, Rochester, NY.

51. Scudder, *Socialism and Character*, 316.

52. Ibid., 332.

53. Ibid., 350.

54. Scudder, *On Journey*, 371.

55. Scudder, *Socialism and Character*, 353.

56. Scudder, "Socialism and Spiritual Progress," 13.

~2~
Vida Dutton Scudder's Theological Vision

Walter Rauschenbusch opened the first chapter to *A Theology for the Social Gospel* with these words: "We have a Social Gospel. We need a systematic theology large enough to match it and vital enough to back it."[1] For Rauschenbusch, the Social Gospel movement needed a viable intellectual basis to make it effective, and theology needed the stimulus and energy of vital social movements. With the same sense of urgency that Rauschenbusch expressed, Vida Dutton Scudder explored the meaning and relevance of her Anglo-Catholic faith for the problems that the modern situation set before her generation. For Scudder, the doctrine, traditions, and rituals of sacramental churches provided the best lens through which Christians could view the changes that needed to take place within the social order. Gary Dorrien pointed out that in Scudder's mind individualism was "intrinsic to Protestantism, but the high sacramental churches were holistic and solidaristic."[2] Congruent with an Anglo-Catholic social conception of divine nature, Scudder thought the best symbol to represent God's loving nature and model for Christian social practice was the Trinity or "Divine Society."

Scholars refer to Rauschenbusch's theology as the guide for identifying the features of Social Gospel theology and consider Rauschenbusch's understanding of the centrality of the kingdom of God to be of primary importance. Scudder's writings, however, expand our understanding of the Social Gospel theology because her conceptualization of the Trinity precedes and informs her notion of God's kingdom. In her first autobiography, published in 1937, Scudder wrote: "Trinitarian belief became at long last the basic condition of my thinking, and more than that, the rhythm to which feeling and deed have come to move."[3] The image of God seen in the Trinity was cooperative and egalitarian; each one of the three with different but equal purposes promoted the divine whole. Keeping this cooperative vision of the Godhead in mind enlarged Scudder's concept of the kingdom and Jesus' role as the initiator of it. Her description of God in social terms provided the model for the highest social life and furnished the norm for social relationships.

Concepts of God Relevant to the Modern Era

Arguing against rigid theologies, Scudder said it was "absurd"[4] to think that human portraits of God might not change; concepts of God had to evolve to maintain relevance for particular groups of people who lived in specific environments and circumstances. In an article on "Religion and Socialism" penned in 1910, she declared:

> We see with increasing clearness that the great word, God, greatest that mankind has ever uttered, connotes a different concept in every age. The God of nomadic tribes is a tribal chieftain. The God of feudalism, as imaged in the superb mosaic that overlooks ruined Messina from the fallen glory of its shrine, is a masterful feudal overlord. That this conception of ultimate being will be deeply, if subtly, affected by the social forms of the future till it assumes a character which we can only dimly predict, is indubitable.[5]

Several years later in *Social Teachings of the Christian Year* she pointed out that the God worshipped by the disciples of Boniface would not bring to mind the same image as the God worshipped by modern worshippers. Theological concepts and social and economic circumstances in which Christians lived were in constant dialectic. Scudder thought immanental concepts were best suited to provide meaning for people who confronted the challenges of modern society.

Rauschenbusch agreed that Christian ideas of God were connected to particular historical experiences:

> The conception of God held by a social group is a social product. . . . As soon as it becomes the property of a social group, it takes on the qualities of that group. Even if it originated in the mind of a solitary thinker or prophet, as soon as it becomes the property of a social group, it takes on the qualities of the group.[6]

Societies that considered kings as the greatest human beings used courtly language in worship and superimposed a monarchial image on the idea of

God. Rauschenbusch asserted that if the concept of God originated among exploiting classes, then it was "almost certain to contain germs of positive sinfulness."[7] For him, this was a real challenge for the Social Gospel. "The worst form of leaving the naked unclothed, the hungry unfed, and the prisoners uncomforted is to leave men under a despotic conception of God and the universe."[8] Rauschenbusch's task was to uncouple the concept of God from the influence and ideology of exploiting classes. To accomplish this, he aimed to "democratize" the conception of God and articulated a theology that would have been familiar to Jesus and the early Christian community, but also would maintain relevance for the working class.

Although the ever-evolving social situation affected worshippers' conception of God, Scudder never thought that ancient Christian doctrines would become obsolete. Christian doctrine maintained relevance for contemporary society. She confessed that a "creed is not an imprisoning wall, it is a gate, opening on a limitless country which can be entered in no other way."[9] As history progressed, worshippers better understood the doctrines of the Church. In *The Witness of Denial*, Scudder traced the development of cynicism toward religion and asserted: "Above their voices (the voices of doubt) is the undaunted, unchanged confession of the Catholic Church. In this confession are recognized all needs discovered by modern men."[10] She later argued that Christianity could supply even the modern movement of democracy with a "soul." When asked why she was still a Church member despite the Church's failures, she responded, "Because I never yet felt any need which Christianity failed to supply."[11]

Scudder's affirmation of Christian doctrine is not evidence of a tacit acceptance of Christian belief, but a statement of her confidence that the Christian religion is flexible enough to withstand even the most challenging social developments. Scudder believed that the "religious life never suffers one to stand still."[12] Religious folks had to continue to interpret the meaning of the creeds within their own contexts and in reference to specific circumstances. As a historic religion, Christianity showed the versatility and adaptability needed to introduce believers to a God who willingly confronted ever-evolving, messy human situations.

Scudder viewed the human journey as an "adventure" or a "quest" through a spiritual landscape in search of union with the Eternal.[13] The quest involved searching for the "Ever-present" God who was active in and discernible through natural and worldly affairs. Martha Boonin-Vail described Scudder's spirituality as one of "boundless inquiry."[14] Scudder discerned God's revelation of Godself in natural and worldly affairs as abundant love.

God's love is so abundant that it flows beyond the Godhead to the open hearts of humanity. Boonin-Vail suggested that Scudder's "theological expressions were essentially an attempt not to bind in that boundlessness or to deny it, but to articulate boundlessness in a religious vocabulary."[15]

Understanding her faith in God as dynamic freed Scudder to draw upon a variety of theological concepts and resources. "Every definition of 'God' that I have ever met is helpful to me," she wrote. "Sometimes in prayer I escape the convention of those three letters by changing the word. 'Deus Meus et Omnia!' I cry with Francis. 'Theos'—the Russian 'Bog'—the Indian 'Brahm' (sic)—'Allah illa Allah!': to one devoutly brooding, the Nameless One draws near; and I bow before Him Who says in the supreme words of revelation, 'I Am That I Am.'"[16] Terms like Alfred North Whitehead's "Deity in Process" and Aristotle's "Unmoved Mover" proved to be instructive descriptions of God for Scudder. Only one name for God seemed ill-suited for her because she had missed the experience that would enable her to connect with this language. In her words, "I cannot with any personal comfort or reality say 'Our Father.' I am very sorry about this. I think the trouble may be that I never knew, and never missed, my earthly father."[17]

Immanental concepts of God spoke most directly to a society driven by the rapid growth of industrial democracy in the modern era.

> As the People have been coming to their own, the visible emblems of King or Judge or even of Father, which had sufficed monarchical and autocratic times, as all religious art can testify, have lost reality. They have been replaced more and more by a burning intuition of a Presence closer than breathing, nearer than hands and feet.[18]

Eastern religions, especially Hinduism, informed her understanding of God's immanence. Scudder liked to think that baby memories had something to do with her sympathies for the political and social revival of India. Childhood memories of India, however, were not the only factors that contributed to her indelible interest in Hinduism. On many occasions she perused her father's library, which had a copy of Max Müller's translation of the Bhagavad Gita. Young Vida read and reread the book until "its contemplative wisdom had sunk into [her] very being."[19] Scudder shared the Hindu belief in the encounter with God through mystical union.[20] Through human relationships and the contemplation of "one or another spiritual landscape,"[21] she thought herself to be pushed toward a greater consciousness of God.

A Social Mystic

When describing herself, Scudder never claimed the term "mystic." "I read the mystics as much as I dared," she admitted, "but mystical experience has rarely if ever been granted my analytical mind."[22] However, she used terms that resonate with the mystical experiences of saints such as Francis of Assisi and Catherine of Siena. She described the religious quest as union with "Infinite Love." Openness to the "overflowing love of God"[23] inspired Christians to break down barriers that separate sacred from profane, material from spiritual, natural from supernatural, and to envision a new social life open to economic and spiritual equality.

For Scudder, the natural order was revelatory and symbolic of God's omnipresence. "Final Reality that controls the secret thought is no distant Monarch, the natural ruler of a world aristocratically organized, but a pervading Spirit, so manifest in the life of nature and the social whole that it is easy to confuse Him with that very world which He inspires."[24] With her sisters of the Society of Companions of the Holy Cross in mind, Scudder wrote: "The rhythm of movement and design which I discern in the natural order is impossible for me to conceive as other than the language of the Divine Mind."[25] The rhythm and beauty in the diversity and profusion of color evident in the natural order revealed nothing other than God's all-pervading nature and creativity in ordering the world.

Let us briefly consider what Scudder meant by using terms that one might associate with nature and science. To describe God, she often employs language suggestive of the cutting-edge scientific discoveries made during her lifetime. In her early works, the terminology that she uses brings to mind Charles Darwin's theories. She describes God's actions in terms of the "rhythm of nature," "natural order," "evolution," "gradual progress," and "growth." Later writings refer to important scientific discoveries and employ language reminiscent of those milestones.

When considering Scudder's articulation of God's vision for a cooperative society, her use of these terms did not parallel the meaning scientists, especially Darwin, gave them. Darwin's thesis defined the law of nature as the survival of the fittest. He introduced the idea that the adaptation of species to their natural environment was random and disconnected from some understanding of God's definitive purpose for the universe. When Scudder linked terms identified with evolution to her concept of God, she was not describing the survival of the fittest by natural competition, but her understanding of the rhythm of God's love.

In his biography of Walter Rauschenbusch, Christopher Evans rightly observed that the acceptance of and even the embrace of natural sciences by Social Gospelers evidenced the interconnection between Social Gospel thought and theological liberalism.[26] Evans said that Rauschenbusch drew upon a wide variety of intellectual resources, including social sciences and natural sciences as well as theological discussions, and integrated these ideas into the conviction that "the social order . . . could be made over to reflect the true intent and purpose of primitive Christianity."[27] Scudder's use of language associated with nature and science illustrates her intent for theological ideas to keep pace with social advances. She did not think that science was antagonistic to religious belief; rather, scientific discoveries appealed to the human imagination and left her in awe of the vastness and mystery of the universe. Washington Gladden, an early proponent of the Social Gospel, also thought that new developments in the scientific disciplines deepened one's understanding of God:

> This modern science which has been supposed by some persons to have banished God from the universe, has not, then, banished order from the universe; it has given us revelations of the order and system which pervades the whole far more impressive than our fathers ever saw.[28]

Like Gladden, Scudder interpreted scientific discoveries through theological lenses. The natural world was symbolic and sacramental; it spoke directly of God's creativity and active involvement in the world:

> For gazing into my valley, wholly passive, abandoned, I will say once more, to contemplation, the blossoming world and the lights and shadows sweeping over the mountain slopes spoke to me directly of Creative Love and Eternal Law. The rhythm that pervades and controls the seemingly confused opulence in the natural order could be no accident.[29]

Although scientific discoveries inspired human imagination, Scudder thought science would never fully be able to explicate "Reality" beyond the material world. "Ultimate Reality? No, that was never yet found by mortal mind. The provisional character of all we claim to 'know' either through our senses or our mind is something we can't escape. There is a waiting boundary, a frontier never to be crossed while we are imprisoned in the natural order."[30]

Christians had an entrance to understand the natural order beyond the doors opened by scientific methodologies. "Outside that area of experience opened, permeated and controlled by our holy faith, we recognize the natural order in which we live, move and have our being, to be not only symbolic but [also] sacramental."[31] Furthermore, science was insufficient to provide the kind of moral sense needed to inform communities prone to misuse their power and discoveries. Christian belief was more apt to offer the dynamic power to discern some sense of greater Reality within the natural order than were "our own senses, our minds, or scientific research."[32]

Scudder's understanding of God's revelation in the natural world evidences her panentheistic perspective. She emphasized the link that one's experience of God within nature provided between natural and supernatural realities. Other Social Gospelers shared this view. Gladden said that God revealed Godself in the laws and forces of nature and in ordered knowledge of the world.[33] In one of her letters to Rauschenbusch, Scudder called him a "mystic":

> Not for a moment should I think of denying to you the title of Mystic. It is a question of the value placed on one type of mysticism, that which is quite unrelated to our fellow-men. I do profoundly honor and value this special type, believing it to be the root from which the fair flower of human love may spring. You, I think, are unduly afraid of it.[34]

Nature mysticism might have worked its way into their thought from the influence of New England transcendentalism or, in Rauschenbusch's case, through German Pietism. Anglo-Catholics drew much of their spirituality from transcendentalist habits of introspection, interests in mysticism, and meditation. Martha Boonin-Vail argued that "transcendentalism introduced patterns of thought, modes of discourse and a spirituality which Anglo-Catholics later combined with other sources to articulate their own critique of religion and society."[35] Transcendentalists and Anglo-Catholics shared the belief that direct experience of the divine was the primary means of gaining religious truth.[36] They rejected Church hierarchy and criticized Roman Catholic emphasis on the association of mysticism as asceticism and the dualism that it promoted. For both groups, spirituality provided a basis for cultural criticism and enabled their adherents to create significant countercultural forces against individualism and the materialism that seemed to be dissolving the bond of contemporary society. The Anglo-Catholic spirituality familiar to Scudder was an alternative to the evangelicalism that influenced some other Social Gospelers.

Like Scudder, Rauschenbusch recognized the need to link religion and one's experience of God in the natural world.[37] Admittedly, he criticized some types of mysticism in *Theology for the Social Gospel.* "Its danger is that it isolates," he wrote. "In energetic mysticism the soul concentrates on God, shuts out the world, and is conscious only of God and itself."[38] His criticism of mysticism associated with Roman Catholic asceticism was a product of his anti-Catholic sentiments. Scudder discussed her view of Rauschenbusch's anti-Catholic sentiments and his attitude toward mysticism in a letter to him in 1918: "I hate your way of assuming that vital Christianity stopped about 200 A.D. and began again with the Reformation," she wrote. "To me, the Medieval Church bore a far nobler social witness than Protestantism has ever borne. And I also deprecate your suggestion about the dangers of mysticism, and your constant implication that it is an unsocial force. That it often has been so I admit, but look at the splendid political and social consciousness of Dante, of Catherine of Siena and of many others to whom the beatific vision has been the goal of human striving."[39]

We should not take Rauschenbusch's negative comments about mysticism at face value. Early in his pastorate at the Second German Baptist Church in Hell's Kitchen, New York, he and two other young clergy persons, Leighton Williams and Nathaniel Schmidt, formed a group for prayer and study that they later called the "Society of Jesus." Together, they studied the Scriptures and engaged in various spiritual disciplines.[40] Undoubtedly, Rauschenbusch criticized an understanding of mysticism that encouraged Christians to turn their backs on the world. Rauschenbusch's poem "The Little Gate to God" suggests that he and Scudder shared a mystical orientation to their belief in how one encountered God. Through his poetry, Rauschenbusch conveyed his belief that moments of solitude brought peace and contentment and assured him that his activities were a meaningful part of some larger purpose. At the same time, his heightened consciousness of God made him feel more at one with all human beings. A line in his poem reads: "My fellowmen are not far-off and forgotten, but close and strangely dear."[41]

Scudder also criticized religious orders that used their mystical experiences to "set themselves apart from greater life and above it."[42] Their attitude created what she termed a "spiritual aristocracy." The consequence was that ordinary people began to think that their relationship with God was less significant than those committed to following a religious rule. For her, mysticism and social passion were "helpless each without the other."[43] God was known through the nurture of "a kind of double vision" that allowed one "conscious contact with Reality impalpable to sense"[44] and stimulated one's interest in social causes.

Her appreciation for mysticism strengthened her understanding of the connection between the social and the spiritual. Saint Francis and his followers further clarified this linkage for Scudder. For the Franciscans, life in Christ sprang from the fount of the direct intuitive experience of God and demanded social as well as inward renunciations. The love of God met in the contemplative life inspired the "summons to renounce"[45] material possessions. The Franciscans invited Christians to subject themselves to voluntary poverty and coupled their understanding of the love of God with renunciation of worldly goods. Their community contrasted with prevalent types of social organization.

In other words, the kind of mysticism that Scudder endorsed did not draw one away from the world, but strengthened one's connection to it. Neri and Brother John, the protagonists in two of her romance novels, exemplified the type of mysticism that lay behind Scudder's social passion. Both of the characters retreated to a mountaintop to contemplate the role that they would play in their societies. Neri, Catherine of Sienna's cleric, galvanized his energies to work for reform in the Roman Catholic Church atop Mount Ventoux.[46] As the English Franciscan monk Brother John climbed the Apennine Mountains near Assisi, "he felt a fresh harmony between outward and inward, as civilization was left behind."[47] Out of that experience of solitude, John mustered the strength to confront the monks who threatened the security of the Franciscan community and to find his friend Pierre.

The Trinity: A Cooperative Vision of God

In *Socialism and Character*, a book containing the outcome of twenty years of Scudder's thought, she agreed with Phillips Brooks's assessment of the Trinity as the "social thought of God."[48] What the Trinity expressed for Christians was the "superb perception that love was eternal, and belonged in its origin, not to the contingent, the transitory, but to the essence of Infinite Being."[49] The concept of the Three-in-One clearly symbolized God's abiding Reality in "fellowship; not in self-seeking, but in a giving of self to the uttermost; not in personality shut in upon itself, but in an equal interchange of love attaining that highest unity which only differentiation can produce."[50] Laying the groundwork for a model for society based on equality and love, the Trinity had obvious implications for her arguments concerning a mutually beneficial partnership between socialism and Christianity.

As a little girl, Scudder had difficulty comprehending the meaning of the doctrine of the Trinity. Remembering a story from her childhood, she recollected the first time that she had an inkling of what the doctrine meant. Asking her mother to explain the concept of the Three-in-One, Harriet Scudder gently chided Vida: "You must wait. You will understand when you are bigger." After a few days young Vida clasped a three-cent coin and queried, "Mamma, isn't this one piece of money?" Her mother responded, "Yes, dear." Then with a hop and a skip Vida exclaimed, "Mamma, I understand the Trinity."[51]

Harriet was right. Young Vida did not really understand the doctrine until she was much "bigger." As she aged, the Trinity bore weighty implications for her social ethic. She underscored its significance in *My Quest for Reality*: "It is with deep humility that I speak of my slowly growing assurance that the best result of the Quest, the best human access to Reality, is offered by the paradoxically comprehensive Trinitarian doctrine presented in the Christian creeds."[52] Drawing upon Scripture and her knowledge of Church history, her social analysis and her own experiences, Scudder presented an interpretation of the Trinity that described God in social terms. God is not a divine person but rather a member of a Divine Society. The three persons of the Godhead exist together coequally and coeternally. Creator, Christ, and Holy Spirit cooperate together to promote a Divine Society based upon equality and love. The Trinity represents the nature of God's creative life, the highest type of social life, and furnishes the norm for social relationships.

A generation before Scudder, Gladden in *How Much Is Left of the Old Doctrines?* pointed out the importance of reinterpreting the doctrine of the Trinity for modern life. Using Jonathan Edwards's "Observations upon the Trinity" as an example, Gladden argued that inherited interpretations of the Trinity had placed too great an emphasis on the personality of God. Edwards spoke of divine persons, with God as the head, covenanting and contracting together to do the work of redemption.[53] Rather than stressing divine "persons," modern interpretations of the Trinity laid emphasis on the ethical relations between the three. He declared that recently "we are beginning . . . to understand that no man can be man alone. It was only in the right relations with others that he realizes himself. And if man was made in the image of God, there must have been some such ethical relations as this in God himself."[54] This was also Scudder's discovery.

Scudder's clearest statement of her understanding of this doctrine is found in *Social Teachings of the Christian Year*. Here, in her analysis of the social message pervading the liturgies of the Anglican prayer book, she described the power of the Church's social instinct. Inspired by her belief that a new world order was on the way, Scudder thought that humanity could safely accomplish imminent changes in society only if religion provided them with a soul. *The Social Teachings of the Christian Year* showed how religion might become the "soul" of social revolution by highlighting the ability of the Christian faith to "inspire new creation." For Scudder, the very existence of the Church year witnessed to the social instinct of the Christian faith. This social instinct carried through into her theological system.

As the dramatic center and climax of the Church year, the liturgies of Trinity-tide introduced worshippers to the meaning of divine nature for the current social context. Interpreting the Trinity in light of contemporary discussions of democracy, Scudder argued that it was "only today, as democracy comes to its own, that these meanings can be fully perceived."[55] The symbol of the Trinity "as found in that glorious Athanasian Hymn of Praise, is the noblest expression of man's best and richest religious thought which has ever yet been evolved."[56] What Athanasius won in his fight for *homoousion* was a social creed teaching that "social harmony depends not on differentiation of rank but on diversity of function."[57] Ancient doctrine still bore the promise to inspire Christians to saturate the world with democracy.[58]

Scudder defined democracy in an article that commented on the conditions of the working class and the failure of democracy in the United States to secure equality for them. Under the current conditions in the United States, people lived under the same governments and institutions but moved in different worlds. The democracy that she hoped for was of another sort, one linked to a spiritual democracy where attitudes were transformed. She said, "If democracy means anything more than mob rule, it means a moral responsibility on the part of its every member consciously to cooperate in the creation of a noble national life."[59] Democracy had the potential to shape the nation into a "harmonious whole."[60] Social harmony would be born from the change of consciousness as individuals turned toward God.

The doctrine of the Trinity showed how far religious thought had the potential to progress because it corresponded to the experience of humanity, pressed home the nature of the Eternal, and had practical implications. Based not only on the authority of Scripture or on the testimony of the creeds, it was a doctrine that "comprehends marvelously all elements which have been vital at any stage of race-experience."[61] Results of laboratory experiments verified the value of the Trinity for modern life. Scientists' conclusions regarding the interdependence and unity of life confirmed that the natural world reflected God's image.

> Our own being, if we look within, is multiplex, though the whirl of concentric personalities apparently, under conditions of health, focuses on one centre. Here is a mystery into which at our present stage of knowledge it is dangerous for most of us to peer; but psychology, no less than metaphysics and science, drives us to recognize that Unity is not so simple a matter as naif speculation assumes.[62]

The complexity of life, the natures of divine and human personalities, could be best expressed in terms of the Many-yet-One, One-yet-Manyness.

Scudder thought the three aspects of God were interdependent, existing together coequally and coeternally. The reality contemplated in the Trinity pressed home the nature of the Eternal and was known as a loving relationship. "Deity is no bright solitude, but the scene of mutual affection."[63] The perpetual exchange of love flowing through and from the Godhead was only possible between equals. In an interactive relationship between God-humanity-world, God engaged humanity through the reconciling ministry of Jesus and acted as the creative force moving through the Spirit. "Deity contains forever the mighty flow and movement of an infinite Life of responding interacting Love."[64] Scudder did not introduce a cold, aloof, transcendent God who related to humanity in terms of domination. She presented a God active in, and responsive to, the world in terms of loving relationship.

Viewing the nature of God in terms of a loving relationship had radical implications for her social ethic. God's love flowed beyond the Godhead by initiating a response to God's engagement of the world. The final relationship between God and humanity was through re-creation; it could no longer be understood in individualistic terms. The meaning of Jesus' sacrificial love was clarified in relation to Divine Society. Sacrificial love was the basis for social organization. Love, Scudder argued, was not given ultimate meaning in care for oneself but in care for others who were unloved.

What it meant to be fashioned in the image of God no longer related only to the state of an individual; we could also think of it in social terms. In the words of Phillips Brooks, "The Christian ideal is not a Divine Person, but a Divine Society."[65] What "the Christian mind sees here at lowest is the assumption that the idea of God is the norm by which human society must be shaped, the type to which it must ultimately conform."[66] Movement toward such a society would progress gradually, but Christians should make this their ultimate task. Participating in the social functions of God—Creating, Redeeming, and Sanctifying—was "human business."[67] Scudder suggested that the Trinity was "the unrecognized witness to democracy."[68]

Its value was uncovered because of humanity's newfound discovery of the evils of social inequalities as brought out in discussions concerning the ideal of the Cooperative Commonwealth. In her mind, the Christian task was "to evolve a society which shall subsist in a unity of love that shall bear some likeness to the Divine Nature in Whose Image we are made."[69]

Understood in relation to the evolution of democratic thought, the ancient doctrine of the Trinity depicted the nature of God's creative life, the highest social life, and furnished a norm for social relationships. Scudder clarified the meaning and relevance of Trinitarian doctrine for Christian social practice. The Trinity provided the model through which Christians could more fully understand what it meant for human beings to be made in God's image and how individuals and society could more closely approximate God's cooperative image by embodying equality and solidarity.

Christ

Each member of the Trinity played an equal but different role in the Divine Society. God was the abundant love interacting with and flowing into open hearts. In Christ, Scudder witnessed God's union with humanity. She believed that God's descent made it possible for human beings to ascend "into union with the Eternal."[70] Jesus helped the disciples to interpret that spiritual ascent in social terms. Teaching the disciples through his comments on the kingdom of God and through his actions by suffering for the sake of others, Jesus showed the union of God with the natural order and the procession of the Holy Spirit. Acting as a social reformer, Jesus defied worldly values. Through his teachings about the kingdom, he connected inward spirituality to the social whole. Jesus' own union with God's infinite love motivated his convictions and actions. Jesus revealed the work of the Trinity in the temporal process.

Jesus and His Teachings about the Kingdom of God

In *Socialism and Character*, Scudder argued that Jesus' concept of the kingdom remained consistent with the social concern of the prophets, but enlarged their national hope. Through the kingdom concept Jesus invited his disciples to further "Divine Society" by encouraging them to find the meaning of the kingdom in the connection between the individual and the social whole. Understood in light of the events of Jesus' life, the kingdom would flower through both evolutionary and revolutionary means.

Agreeing with the comments Rauschenbusch made at the beginning of *Christianity and the Social Crisis*, Scudder thought, "We are better equipped to comprehend what manner of man he (Jesus) was, and to what end he lived, than any generation since his contemporaries."[71] The Bible shared in a "new social reinterpretation"[72] encouraged by modern approaches to history. Rauschenbusch drew upon the work of scholars such as Shailer Mathews, Ernest Renan, Emil Schürer, and Julius Wellhausen. Their advances in biblical study enabled Rauschenbusch to set Jesus within his own context, to see his religion and ministry in line with the prophets, and to identify his purpose to advance the kingdom of God.

Scudder thought that only with the recent recognition of the centrality of the kingdom in Jesus' teachings had Christians taken the opportunity to understand his importance. Attributing this theological breakthrough to Rauschenbusch, Scudder wrote, "The greatest religious gain of our own day is the rediscovery of this 'dear truth,' as Dr. Rauschenbusch loved to call it."[73] Like Rauschenbusch, she thought that returning the kingdom to its rightful place in Christian theology was of vital importance. For Rauschenbusch, the coming of the kingdom meant "the partial and earthly realization of divine society."[74] Scudder described Jesus as the "chief social idealist,"[75] who fought even unto death to ensure social revolution. They agreed that the kingdom would come through personal renewal, but not for the sake of individual "souls."

> Jesus worked on individuals and through individuals, but his real end was not individualistic but social, and in his method he employed strong social forces. He knew that a new view of life would have to be implanted before the new life could be lived and that the new society would have to nucleate around personal centers of renewal. But his end was not the new soul, but the new society; not man, but Man.[76]

Both grounded the kingdom in the social and natural conditions of humanity. But, perhaps more strongly than Rauschenbusch, Scudder focused on a notion of the kingdom as incarnate within all souls. The kingdom of God within us did not sanction a life of luxury,[77] but warranted the Christian choice for simplicity. She connected the kingdom concept to a change in attitude of individuals and with specific changes in society. The kingdom was not a utopian place, but a state of God consciousness that empowered social change. Scudder disconnected the kingdom concept from material gain by linking it with the inner self.

Various interpretations of what Jesus meant by the kingdom of God had developed throughout Christian history. Opposing popular interpretations of the kingdom, Scudder opted for a social conception. Protestants viewed his teaching in relation to the individual soul as "a personal, wholly inward matter."[78] Catholics equated the Church with the kingdom. Scudder disagreed with both views.

Discarding the Protestant view, she argued that Jesus "illumined and enlarged"[79] the concept of the kingdom rather than replacing it with something radically different. "In his day the mention of the Kingdom evoked to every Jewish breast a social and visible conception."[80] Jesus' contemporaries clearly connected the kingdom with messianic hope. Remembering Mary's sweet song, the Magnificat, Scudder said that Jesus' followers understood the kingdom as "the reign of justice and social equality, the satisfaction of the hungry, the exaltation of the poor, while the powerful should be degraded and the rich sent empty away."[81] Jesus endorsed this teaching and enlarged it by emphasizing "spirituality and inwardness."[82] Through his teachings about the kingdom,

> he modifies crude contemporary ideas, he ratifies the faith of his people that a visible society, holy unto the Lord, is the ideal for which they are to work and pray. His teaching consistently aims to create not mystics nor recluses, but brothers.[83]

Neither could the ecclesiastical conception of the kingdom encompass Jesus' teachings. Scudder wrote, "The thought of the Kingdom is [as] large as the liberal air: intimate study of later phrases makes clear that the Church is never to be an end in itself."[84] Only a third or social conception of the kingdom would satisfactorily fit with Jesus' teachings.

The Sermon on the Mount was the key to understanding Jesus' ideal of the kingdom. On that grassy hill, Jesus presented the ideal of the kingdom as fellowship, not self-seeking. In his sermon Jesus counseled his followers to follow two principles, to live conspicuous lives so that "their good works may be seen and God be glorified"[85] and to fulfill the moral precepts of the past. Jesus' notion of the kingdom was broader than personal and ecclesiastical conceptions because it stressed both inward spirituality and the relationship of the individual to the social whole.

> The Sermon is deeply and intimately personal, for only a humanity born "from within" can sustain a regenerate state. But to construe this stress on

> the personal life into indifference to the social whole, and to think that one loves one's neighbor as one's self and fulfills the Law by an attitude of passive amiability toward the world and ardent tenderness toward one's family, is strangely to misread the Master's mind. Life in the society he contemplates has its wellspring in the heart; but the waters are to flow forth for the healing of the nations.[86]

Answering the question of whether or not the kingdom was of time or eternity, Scudder placed the kingdom squarely in both time and eternity. In her kingdom concept, eternity entered into time through both evolutionary and revolutionary means. Early in his career, she pointed out, Jesus used organic metaphors to describe the kingdom in his parables:

> The sown field, the mustard tree, expanding from tiny atom of organic life till the birds take shelter in its branches, the seed growing secretly, . . . these are the homely, vital parallels used to suggest the advance of the Kingdom of God.[87]

The Kingdom would progress slowly, like a mustard seed or a seed sown in fertile soil. She observed that in the middle of his life, Jesus changed his point of view. Moving away from the politicization of his message made by the crowds, "he altered the whole tone of his teaching and turned from public instruction to the training of a small group."[88] His teachings showed a new emphasis on judgment. He sent out the disciples with the message that the kingdom would not be achieved by political means and "would never fulfill their provincial hopes."[89] Jesus enlarged the expectations of the Jewish people and expanded their notion of hope beyond provincial and national boundaries. The kingdom was to come on earth, not to be limited to a few privileged regions. "Now the point of view has changed, and the Kingdom is to be ushered in by convulsion and crisis. The destruction of nations, the upheaval of nature, the strange invasion of time by eternity, are its precursors."[90] Eternity now entered into time by revolutionary means. The cross then took central place in the progress of the kingdom.

> It rises not at the end but in the middle of the drama. Jesus placed it at its true historic point when he environed his followers with eternity, insisting at the same time that the farthest fulfillment of his dream of brotherhood in an eternal future was no mere phantom nor promise of heavenly consolation for the individual, but a Kingdom of effective justice to be possessed on earth by bodily men.[91]

Describing the meaning of the cross in *Social Teachings of the Christian Year*, Scudder called the cross "the consummation of the religion of the Incarnation—here, where the Infinite is revealed at the last stage of its self-emptying which is its true fulfillment, claiming every prerogative of finiteness."[92] In "The Cross in Utopia," Scudder said that she thought it was a mistake for her contemporaries to emphasize Jesus' life and ministry as opposed to the cross. The Gospels, she pointed out, dedicated one-fourth to one-third of their text to the passion narrative. There was no need to apologize for God's activity. She affirmed that the suffering God was the Christian answer to rebellious human agony.

Jesus' Sacrifice and What His Suffering Meant

Scudder was anxiously aware that for Christians to view the cross as the center of history raised significant questions about the meaning of Jesus' suffering. Since the end of the Civil War, American Protestants for the most part believed that eliminating the suffering of the poor was both impossible and even undesirable. The prevailing attitude toward the poor was that the poor controlled their own destinies. They were poor because of their own laziness and depraved behavior. If the poor worked harder, then they would get ahead.[93] Interpreting the significance of suffering in light of her context, she viewed Jesus' suffering in reference to the suffering of those oppressed by the hands of greedy industrialists. Scudder wondered if Christians could see Jesus' sacrifice as relevant to modern society without making martyrs of the suffering of those marginalized by the capitalist system. Could one argue for alleviating the suffering of society's poor without minimizing the importance of Jesus' suffering and sacrificial love? Scudder recognized suffering as an important theme in the Christian story, but she did not believe that the cross validated involuntary human anguish. She avoided this pitfall by underscoring both the voluntary aspect of Jesus' sacrifice and his willingness to endure pain for the sake of others. The theory of atonement that she etched out was not substitutionary. Christ suffered voluntarily for the greater goal of reconstructing a society based on harmony with divine nature. Jesus did not finish the job of bringing the social order back into sync with God's natural rhythm. Redemption was not a completed act, but a gradual, continual process advanced by the activity of human hands motivated by God's love. The cross pointed toward God's involvement in history and God's willingness to work in cooperation with humanity.

In *Social Teachings of the Christian Year*, Scudder found two aspects of Jesus' suffering of deep social significance: his voluntary sacrifice and his willingness to endure physical pain. Jesus voluntarily rejected worldly standards and values of love. "Jesus never courted death. That His Agony has redemptive value is deep and mystic truth, but He did not live to die, as Roman teaching has sometimes assumed; He lived to establish the Kingdom of God."[94] Jesus embodied revolutionary forces by rejecting the Church and the state. Scudder thought that he chose to be crucified because he "wanted to carry out His purpose, . . . because He saw that He was not to be permitted to do so in the way that He had hoped."[95] Though crucified as a common criminal, Christ died as a savior, not as a victim. The cross showed the great reformer's "defiance of the existing social and religious order."[96]

Not only did Jesus voluntarily sacrifice himself in defiance of worldly values; he also willingly endured pain for the sake of others. In Jesus' pain, the suffering of the innocent no longer seemed futile. "By the divine paradox of the Cross we know that these experiences may not be ignominious waste, but may connote the richest productive and creative values."[97] The story of Christ's passion showed God's dealings with humanity. In the atonement, the world witnessed God's double attitude toward it. Through the crucifixion God showed both a willingness to be one with the world and God's intent to defy worldly values. Out of Christ's inward journey toward voluntarily sacrificing himself for the sake of others and his willing identification with human pain, social transformation could be born.

The cross—by avoiding an emphasis on private morality and expressing the deeper reality of the cooperation between God and humanity to redeem the social order—had redemptive meaning for Scudder's social context. Change in society would not come without cost. If the world wanted real democracy, then corporate sacrifices would be necessary. Scudder began with three suggestions: sacrifice of class, sacrifice of nation, and sacrifice of Church.[98]

In a later article, "The Cross in Utopia," Scudder asserted that the cross "reveals the Nature of the Deity, which the nature of humanity must reproduce."[99] Discarding the doctrine of substitutionary atonement, Scudder refused to interpret the atonement as an "accomplished transaction."[100] Rather, she understood atonement as an ongoing process. Human beings were called to enter into God's redemptive process by responding willingly to Jesus' voluntary sacrifice.

> Man entering into that process, conformed to that law, may in his turn redeem. The cross is the ground-plan of the universe; and the way of the cross for all followers of the Crucified is the only pathway from illusion to reality; the one way of life and peace.[101]

Perhaps more clearly stated in the "Waiting Task," Scudder viewed the cross and passion as more than an event in time; it is a way of informing humanity of God's law:

> Sacrifice must be perceived to be the law for the healthful Christian state as well as for the healthful individual. This social reading of the doctrine of the Atonement reveals the constant methods of God in history, to a world which, ignoring or neglecting His laws, can but crucify Him afresh. Christ is the Revealer; but the Revealer is also the Redeemer, and as His redeemed follow with Him the Way of the Cross among the dimness of the nations, they shall find it indeed the Way of Life and Peace.[102]

She called upon Christians to reproduce God's law in civilization. Reproducing that law would restore the rhythm of the universe.

When writing "The Cross in Utopia," Scudder realized that her position might present a problem when considering what she advocated regarding the establishment of a more just society. As a Christian Socialist, she asserted that God invited society to eliminate the destruction of the forces behind poverty, greed, and inequality. But if society eliminated these forces, would the significance of the cross be lost for Christians? A wicked society crucified Jesus. Injustice created the conditions in which we could better understand God's creative act of redemption. If a more egalitarian society was established, then would the cross become irrelevant? In addition, too many traditions pointed to poverty as a vehicle through which one might encounter God. If suffering was a means to understand God's infinite love, then would the elimination of suffering cut off one's access to God? Scudder concluded the followers of Christ could not discard the importance of suffering. Instead, one must discriminate as to what suffering purported. Christians must work against certain types of suffering, but the suffering identified with Christ might still be thought of as life-giving.

Certain types of suffering encouraged social creativity, and she would not abandon them even in her egalitarian vision of society. In the "Cross in Utopia," Scudder said that physical suffering could profit the soul. For example, those who chose to involve themselves in social activism would suffer. They, however, suffered voluntarily for the sake of achieving a better society. The suffering of others also evoked a kind of social creativity. Quoting William Blake, she made her case plain:

> Mercy could be no more
> If there were nobody poor;
> And pity not more could be
> If all were as happy as we.[103]

The soul profited by feelings of mercy that were prompted by the sufferings of others.

On the other hand, society must fight the suffering that suffocates the soul. Scudder identified this type of suffering as involuntary. Unemployed workers, those living in crowded tenement housing, and those worn out by long hours of standing on the factory floors—all these were stifled by their living conditions. Victimized by their need to secure basic material necessities, those who suffered involuntarily could not even free themselves to contemplate God's greater reality active in their lives.

Other Social Gospelers showed equal concern for how Christian interpretations of Christ's suffering affected the plight of the poor. Whereas Scudder connected suffering to changes in individual attitudes and their influence upon the social whole, Rauschenbusch addressed the issue in a slightly different tone of voice. Interpreting the value of suffering in solidaristic terms, he wrote, "Social suffering serves social healing."[104] Like physical pain, social suffering warned society of the existence of abnormal conditions and had the potential to set the entire body in motion to heal itself. Reverdy Ransom, bishop of the African Methodist Episcopal Church, thought that God would use the suffering of African-Americans to prepare them to do great things:

> Their preparation and their training lay through the paths that led by way of the slave pen and the auction block, in fugitive wanderings under the dim North Star where baying bloodhounds lurked. In pain and agony they came through Ku Klux Klan, through the lynchers' ruthless violence of wanton murder and fiendish orgies of burning at the stake while upon all these barbarities were heaped the dehumanizing programs of American Jim Crowism.
>
> "If the vision tarry, wait for it." But waiting does not mean inaction, to do nothing, to stand still. Those who wait upon God work ceaselessly for the fulfillment of the vision toward which they strive. So these

> Americans of African descent, while waiting have been serving their apprenticeships in preparation for the great role they are to play in the consummation of God's plans.[105]

Rauschenbusch, Ransom, and Scudder agreed: God hoped that the world's attitude toward suffering would change. They also thought that those who knew suffering firsthand could draw upon their alienating and sometimes painful experiences when mustering their energies to work for a better society. In Scudder's view, society would not totally eliminate suffering but would rid itself of all enforced miseries. Suffering would not cease but would more truly reflect the redemptive qualities known in the suffering of Christ. "If we want to become more fully alive," she wrote, "we must consent to be more hurt. As we advance to higher levels in the corporate life, as we shake off the clogs that drag our steps, we may expect to meet new sources of joy, but we may also expect to suffer more."[106]

The Church and the World

Faith in the incarnation was to know the "experience of the divine working through the human."[107] As third in the procession of the Trinity, the Spirit functioned to stir the memories of believers about what Christ taught. Scudder thought it significant that the Spirit appeared third in the sequence of the Trinity because this "protects the dignity and primacy of human character."[108] Proceeding from the "Father" and the "Son" secured human reverence for one's moral nature.

In *Social Teachings of the Christian Year*, Scudder discussed the Holy Spirit in her study of the social significance of Pentecost. During the season of Whitsuntide, the Church centered its thought on God the Indweller, God within us. Through God's activity of coming "as the Paraclete, the Comforter, the sweet Guest of the Soul,"[109] God revealed human beings to be the instruments of democracy. A faith enlivened by the Spirit became "the final sanction and seal of democracy."[110] The Spirit inspired individuals to put on an attitude like that of Christ. Scudder connected the right attitude to relinquishing ownership of private property and the pursuit of Christian democracy. She did not limit the work of the Spirit to transforming the attitudes of individuals. Evidence of the first experience of Pentecost showed that the infant Christian community expressed the gift of the Spirit not only in the change of individual attitudes but also through its communal life.

Spirit-Inspired Community

Scudder observed that the indwelling of the Spirit in the Church celebrated on that first Pentecost also initiated the outward expression of spiritual gifts. Boundaries set by human hearts or the Church's walls could not hold the Spirit captive. The Spirit flowed outward. Whitsun season reminded churchgoers of how the early Christian community responded to the outflowing of the Spirit. They created a limitless democracy in Christ. The Christian community understood itself as contrasting with worldly values.

Recalling the story of Pentecost recorded in Acts, Scudder recognized that the Spirit gifted the early community with tongues. The first community received the power to make itself more widely understood and was unable to keep quiet about the gift its members had received. Scudder interpreted this gift in light of the modern context; to speak in tongues meant to learn the language of others. "The ability to make oneself understood, not by forcing or even urging other people to learn our language, but by talking to them in their own."[111] She expressed her concern for the working class, those excluded by the established Church, by making an opening for discussions with them:

> Whether we look at the corporate Church or at our private behavior, it seems equally forgotten that this is what the Spirit must do for us. As a rule, the idea is twisted completely round. Every man and every class is content to shout its shibboleth at its adversary, hoping to convince him by deafening him. So capital addresses labor, so labor capital; so even the Christian Church tries to coax the unchurched to come and learn her ways and speak her tongue, rarely indeed trying the other way.[112]

The Spirit broke down barriers of class and nation. All were equally able to understand God's revelation. Scudder hoped that the same Spirit would grant the gift for each to understand the language of the other and bear a new sense of internationalism in the world.

Continuing her reading in Acts, Scudder saw that the next result was the creation of a community based on the Spirit's inspiration. The first community set itself apart by holding all things in common: faith, hope, zeal, and most important, property.

> Now the whole group of those who believed were of one heart and soul, and no one claimed private ownership of any possessions, but everything they

> own was held in common. With great power the apostles gave their testimony to the resurrection of the Lord Jesus, and great grace was upon them all. There was not a needy person among them, for as many as owned lands or houses sold them and brought the proceeds of what was sold. They laid it at the apostles' feet, and it was distributed to each as any had need. (Acts 4:32–35 NRSV)

From their attitude toward property, Scudder surmised that the infant Christian community organized itself for the mutual benefit of all instead of limiting itself to prayer meetings. The first Pentecostal adventure was that the "Holy Ghost leads the Church straight to distinctive self-expression concerning worldly wealth and social relationships and that the right attitude toward property is a primary object of Christian solicitude."[113]

Democratic Impulse in the Church

Empowered by the Spirit, the first Christians realized that a greater sense of Reality resided within the community of believers. This belief empowered them to view themselves as God's instruments and to work to fashion their environment in the likeness of that greater Reality. The same Spirit manifest in the life of humanity breathed life into the earliest community of believers. From its birth the Church was "the instrument of that democracy through which the Indwelling Spirit is to work out His blessed will."[114] Fully aware of the implications of her belief in relation to the behavior of the Church in recent years, Scudder carefully dealt with the reality of the Church's many failures. Although the Church had made mistakes, she pointed out that its basic character was democratic.

Scudder's optimism rang loud in her discussion of the Church as an instrument of democracy. Throughout history the Church held to its democratic purpose almost in spite of itself. Within the Church we can find evidence of the Spirit of equality despite the Church's apparent shortcomings. Scudder recognized that some movements in Christian history stood out in support of maintaining a disparity between Church and world. The Church fathers Clement, Ambrose, Tertullian, and Augustine upheld this attitude in their views on private property. The medieval Church benefited from the wealth of the landowners, but it never forgot the value of a positive attitude toward common property. Franciscans and other mendicant orders voluntarily renounced worldly goods. Even though the Church modeled itself as a hierarchy in the Middle Ages, democracy still made a home for itself within the Church's walls. Peasant and noble alike were eligible for its highest honors, saints were drawn from every rank, and monastic life approximated a communist Utopia. She admitted that the Church often repeated its blunders, but "nevertheless she has never wholly forfeited her proud dignity of being the refuge of the humble, the home of the One Family of God."[115] The prayer book always led Christians back to that last gathering of "working-folk" in the upper room. On the night before his betrayal, Jesus sacramentally gave the Spirit to the community surrounding him.

Drawing upon the ideas of Charles Kingsley, Scudder asserted that the sacraments disclosed the democratic impulse in the Church. Baptizing all children, the Church offered the sacrament of equality to infants. As Kingsley wrote, "Every little human being born into London is claimed as being the equal of every other little human being."[116] A sign of true "brotherhood," the Eucharist is to feed all people and the Spirit-inspired Scriptures, "which the Church so jealously guards, are the charter of freedom."[117]

Although she found evidence of the Church living up to its true nature, she was concerned about critics complaining that the gifts of the Spirit shared in the Church came from "fatherly hands." Communicants did not have direct, equal access to the sacraments. Scudder dealt with this issue by interpreting the role of the priest as symbolic of the believer's contact with the divine in fellowship. God entrusted human beings to consecrate the bread and wine; to honor the world in which they lived as sacred. The priest's actions were symbolic of "the silent witness of the church to the union of humanity in God."[118] God was present in the sacraments when "two or three are met,"[119] as the community came together, with members not staying in isolation. She thought of the dispensation of sacraments by the hands of the priest not as a symbol of hierarchy, but of unity; unity in God's family existing in fellowship as opposed to isolation.

Scudder saw the tide of the Spirit ebb in the Reformation, when Protestantism began to flourish. "Protestantism on the whole grew and flourished in the period of lusty individualism."[120] The right attitude toward property remained submerged in history until it surfaced again in the writings of people like Canon Barnett and Rauschenbusch. Through the growing interest in Christianity's social message, the first Pentecostal experience carried a renewed significance for Christians. As the Spirit whispered in modern ears, individuals once again heeded the warning that too great a concern with material things hampered their growth.

Equating the Spirit's activity with antimaterialism, Scudder felt that a collective expression of a Christian attitude toward private property and wealth should be forthcoming. The Spirit moved Christians toward self-control and restrained their passions for material things. An ethic born of the Spirit did not change throughout the ages, but God called the Christian community to adapt itself to express that ethic in the ever-changing social context. The work of the Church was to dig deeply into the mystical recesses of its soul and in light of the Spirit's inspiration to lead the Christian community toward equality. The Spirit kindled fires within the faithful that would be kept burning on the altar of the Church and illumine the world.

If the Church spoke its own distinctive language, the world would never lead the Church. Rather, the Church "is to insist that her children sift theories uncompromisingly in the light of Christian idealism; it is above all to offer the incentive which shall draw men to try the Great Adventure of Christian living in terms of the new age."[121] Christ had given the Church a double commission: to nurture the spiritual journey of its individual members, and to help Christians express that belief in outward action in their own social context. Scudder viewed the mission of the Church to enliven its believers as unalterable, but the Church also needed to continually translate its distinctive voice to speak to the changing social situation. In every age, the Church maintained its vitality by speaking to the most recent social problems.

Notes

1. Walter Rauschenbusch, *A Theology for the Social Gospel* (1917; repr., Louisville: Westminster/John Knox Press, 1997), 1.
2. Gary J. Dorrien, *The Making of American Liberal Theology: Idealism, Realism, and Modernity 1900–1950* (Louisville: Westminster John Knox Press, 2003), 137.
3. Vida Dutton Scudder, *On Journey* (New York: Dutton, 1937), 20.
4. Vida Dutton Scudder, *Social Teachings of the Christian Year* (New York: Dutton, 1921), 220.
5. Vida Dutton Scudder, "Religion and Socialism," *Harvard Theological Review* 3 (April 1910): 242.
6. Rauschenbusch, *A Theology for the Social Gospel*, 167.
7. Ibid., 169.
8. Ibid., 174.
9. Scudder, *On Journey*, 233.
10. Vida Dutton Scudder, *The Witness of Denial* (New York: Dutton, 1895), 139.
11. Vida Dutton Scudder, "Christian and Churchwoman: Why?" *The Living Church* 87 (August 13, 1932): 355.
12. Scudder, *On Journey*, 233.
13. Vida Dutton Scudder, *Socialism and Character* (Boston: Houghton, Mifflin, 1912), 316.
14. Martha Clara Boonin-Vail, "New Wine in Old Bottles: Anglo-Catholicism in the United States, 1840–1919" (PhD diss., Yale University, 1993), 145.

15. Ibid.
16. Scudder, *On Journey*, 363.
17. Ibid.
18. Scudder, *Social Teachings of the Christian Year*, 188.
19. Scudder, *On Journey*, 17.
20. See Vida Dutton Scudder, "The Doubting Pacifist," *The Yale Review* (July 1917): 738–58; and "The Cross in Utopia," *The Hibbert Journal* 32 (October 1933): 56–69, where Scudder referred to the story of Arjuna recorded in the Bhagavad Gita.
21. Scudder, *On Journey*, 362.
22. Ibid., 235–39.
23. Scudder, *Social Teachings of the Christian Year*, 214.
24. Scudder, *Socialism and Character*, 332.
25. Vida Dutton Scudder, *My Quest for Reality* (Wellesley, MA: Printed for the author, 1952), 20.
26. Christopher Evans, *The Kingdom Is Always But Coming: A Life of Walter Rauschenbusch* (Grand Rapids: Eerdmans, 2004), 49.
27. Ibid.
28. Washington Gladden, *Burning Questions of the Life That Now Is, and of That Which Is to Come* (New York: Century, 1890), 28–29.
29. Scudder, *My Quest for Reality*, 21.
30. Ibid., 17.
31. Ibid., 19.
32. Ibid., 21.
33. Washington Gladden, *"How Much Is Left of the Old Doctrines?"* (Boston: Houghton, Mifflin, 1899).
34. Scudder to Rauschenbusch, March 27, 1918. Walter Rauschenbusch Papers, American Baptist Historical Society Manuscript Collection, Samuel Colgate Historical Library, Colgate Rochester Divinity School, Rochester, NY.
35. Boonin-Vail, "New Wine in Old Bottles," 58.
36. Like Transcendentalists, Anglo-Catholics believed that they could directly encounter God's reality. Individuals could experience the supernatural through intuition and actively participated in mystical union when receiving the sacraments. See Boonin-Vail, "New Wine in Old Bottles," 62.
37. Rauschenbusch, *A Theology for the Social Gospel*, 3, 21.
38. Ibid., 103–4.
39. Scudder to Rauschenbusch, February 27, 1918. Walter Rauschenbusch Papers, American Baptist Historical Society Manuscript Collection, Samuel Colgate Historical Library, Colgate Rochester Divinity School, Rochester, NY.
40. Evans, *The Kingdom Is Always But Coming*, 66.
41. Walter Rauschenbusch, "The Little Gate to God." Walter Rauschenbusch Papers, American Baptist Historical Society Manuscript Collection, Samuel Colgate Historical Library, Colgate Rochester Divinity School, Rochester, NY.
42. Journal entry, Journal 1932–1933. Scudder Papers, Sophia Smith Collection, Smith College Archives, Northampton, MA.
43. Vida Dutton Scudder, "Mysticism and Social Passion," *The World Tomorrow* 13 (March 1930): 124.
44. Ibid., 122.
45. Vida Dutton Scudder, *Christian Simplicity* (The Christian Social Union Publication 52; August 15, 1898): 8.

46. Vida Dutton Scudder, *The Disciple of a Saint: Being the Imaginary Biography of Raniero di Landoccio de Pagliaresi* (New York: Dutton; London: Dent, 1907), 201–2.

47. Vida Dutton Scudder, *Brother John: A Tale of the First Franciscans* (Boston: Little, Brown, 1927), 154.

48. Scudder, *Socialism and Character*, 351.

49. Ibid., 352.

50. Ibid.

51. Scudder, *On Journey*, 20.

52. Scudder, *My Quest for Reality*, 45.

53. Gladden, *How Much Is Left of the Old Doctrines?* 135.

54. Ibid., 143.

55. Scudder, *Social Teachings of the Christian Year*, 231.

56. Ibid., 221.

57. Ibid., 231.

58. Ibid., 225.

59. Vida Dutton Scudder, "A Hidden Weakness in Our Democracy," *The Atlantic Monthly* 89 (May 1902): 638.

60. Ibid., 644.

61. Scudder, *Social Teachings of the Christian Year*, 222.

62. Ibid., 223.

63. Ibid., 228.

64. Ibid.

65. Ibid., 229.

66. Ibid., 230.

67. Ibid., 236.

68. Ibid., 233.

69. Ibid., 232.

70. Scudder, *On Journey*, 366.

71. Scudder, *Socialism and Character*, 373.

72. Walter Rauschenbusch, *Christianity and the Social Crisis* (1907; repr., Louisville: Westminster/John Knox Press, 1991), 45.

73. Scudder, *Social Teachings of the Christian Year*, 21.

74. Rauschenbusch, *A Theology for the Social Gospel*, 132.

75. Scudder, *Socialism and Character*, 375.

76. Rauschenbusch, *Christianity and the Social Crisis*, 60–61.

77. Scudder, *Christian Simplicity*, 5.

78. Scudder, *Socialism and Character*, 376.

79. Ibid., 379.

80. Ibid., 377.

81. Ibid., 378.

82. Ibid., 379.

83. Ibid.

84. Ibid., 380.

85. Ibid., 381.

86. Ibid., 383.

87. Ibid., 385–86.

88. Ibid., 388.

89. Ibid., 389.

90. Ibid., 390.

91. Ibid., 394.
92. Scudder, *Social Teachings of the Christian Year*, 136.
93. Henry F. May, *Protestant Churches and Industrial America* (New York: Harper & Bros., 1949), 53–54.
94. Scudder, *Social Teachings of the Christian Year*, 137.
95. Ibid., 138.
96. Ibid., 141.
97. Ibid., 143.
98. Ibid., 148.
99. Scudder, "The Cross in Utopia," 56.
100. Ibid., 56. Also see Vida Dutton Scudder, "The Waiting Task," *Christendom* (London) 1 (June 1931): 121–28.
101. Scudder, "The Cross in Utopia," 56–57.
102. Scudder, "The Waiting Task," 128.
103. Scudder, "The Cross in Utopia," 61.
104. Rauschenbusch, *A Theology for the Social Gospel*, 183.
105. Anthony B. Pinn, ed., *Making the Gospel Plain: The Writings of Bishop Reverdy C. Ransom* (Harrisburg: Trinity Press International, 1999), 219.
106. Scudder, "The Cross in Utopia," 65.
107. Scudder, *Socialism and Character*, 350.
108. Scudder, *Social Teachings of the Christian Year*, 190.
109. Ibid., 188.
110. Ibid., 187.
111. Ibid., 197.
112. Ibid.
113. Ibid., 203.
114. Ibid., 191.
115. Ibid., 193–94.
116. Ibid., 191–92.
117. Ibid.
118. Ibid., 195.
119. Ibid.
120. Ibid., 211.
121. Vida Dutton Scudder, *The Church and the Hour* (New York: Dutton, 1917), 30.

3
Character and the Cooperative Commonwealth

In describing the dismal state of morality under capitalism,[1] Vida Dutton Scudder wrote, "The individual is the center more exclusively than in any preceding phase of history, and the defence of personal rights in an indifferent or hostile world is one first canon of duty."[2] Scudder did not always use the word *sin* to describe human shortcomings; however, her rigorous discussions of the problems facing the modern world revealed her conception of sin. Individualism pervaded social institutions, and self-interest guided individual choices. Too often people subordinated love for others to profits. Economic forces controlled the destinies of the working classes and limited their freedoms. The property-owning elite stored up power for themselves and relegated those without property to live in stifling tenement houses and remain powerless to change their situations. Those left in want experienced not only material poverty, but also spiritual poverty; rarely did the poor have the luxury of time or energy to focus on some sense of reality beyond the social maze. Scudder charged that this individualistic social order impeded the development of moral character and prevented the realization of equality among classes and races as well as between genders. Human practices and institutions fell far short of embodying Divine Society.

The situation disquieted Scudder, but she also believed that individuals, institutions, policies, and practices could be reshaped to create an environment that would facilitate the growth of stronger moral character. The Church had a special charge and investment in modeling and furthering the social changes that needed to occur. Gifted with the language to express God's vision for a cooperative society and challenged by intellectual developments in the social sciences and other fields, the Church was responsible for educating Christians about social dilemmas and preparing them for the emergent social order. At the time, Scudder thought a socialist state had the greatest potential to create an environment where people would rightly understand proper attitude and character. Scudder queried, "There is just one thing we do not talk much about, and that is, supposing the socialist state a fact, supposing we arrive, what sort of men and women shall we be when we get there?"[3] With the Cooperative Commonwealth in view, individual attitudes and communal social practices needed to be transformed. Once realized, the Cooperative Commonwealth would provide an environment in which human beings had greater potential to free themselves from the bondage of materialism and move closer to God by working for the betterment of the human community.

Scudder's understanding of the new world order, the Cooperative Commonwealth, was dependent upon her analysis of the current social circumstances. Although she never provided a detailed blueprint for the Cooperative Commonwealth, Scudder outlined specific attitudes, behaviors, and practices having the potential to create an environment that would nurture stronger moral character. For her generation, she thought that socialist policies were most likely to liberate citizens from economic deprivation and spiritual captivity. In the Cooperative Commonwealth, people would share power. They would consider justice in relation to the common good as opposed to self-interest. People rather than profits would be the end of production. This new world order would enable individuals to focus on their spiritual needs.

Character in a Competitive Environment

Central to her critique was the idea that competition fostered "self-regarding virtues" and "instincts of defiant self-protection."[4] Her economic convictions followed the Fabians, supplemented by Marxist ideology.[5] In this conviction she was somewhat like Richard Ely, George Herron, and Walter Rauschenbusch, who maintained varying degrees of commitment to socialism. Critiquing society on the basis of its economic policies revealed not only its material injustices but also, perhaps more importantly, its spiritual injustices. Capitalism emphasized individual freedom as opposed to freedom in community. These cultural trends ran counter to the principles taught by Jesus in the Beatitudes. Jesus presented the ideal of the kingdom in fellowship, not self-seeking. Society was to bless the poor. They were to know the kingdom of heaven on earth. Those who mourned, the meek, and those who hungered and thirsted for righteousness were to inherit the earth and be filled. In Scudder's social context, Jesus' vision had not been realized. The industrial machine had run over the poor, meek, hungry, and thirsty.

Speaking through Hilda Lathrop's voice in *A Listener in Babel*, Scudder characterized the situation:

> The truth is . . . that there are many kinds of virtues, but only one set has any economic value; and these are, we must admit, not the virtues most emphasized by Christ.[6]

Capitalistic society encouraged social disparities and held its citizens captive to their own individual needs. Contrary to God's vision as taught by Jesus, the industrial revolution rewarded entrepreneurs and wealthy investors.

The Fabian Society was founded to advocate transformation of capitalistic society and to work out the implications of this transformation. A predominately middle-class and well-educated constituency, the Fabians believed that "the necessary instruments of production should be held and organized by the community, instead of by individuals, within or outside of the community."[7] Sidney Webb's *Historic Essay* made a profound impression upon Scudder. Drawing upon the thought of Auguste Comte, Charles Darwin, and Herbert Spencer, Webb asserted that society could no longer think of itself as an unchanging state. These scholars had moved from understanding the social ideal as static to seeing it as something constantly growing and dynamic. Webb interpreted history as a gradual advance toward a truer democracy, and he discussed socialism as part of the incremental but inevitable evolution of democratic ideals. Webb recognized the Fabians as a distinct socialist organization because they realized that organic changes in society would occur if they were democratic, accepted by the majority; gradual, with the masses not regarding them as immoral; and at least within the English context, constitutional and peaceful.[8]

Early in the twentieth century, three strains of socialism—represented by Giuseppe Mazzini, Karl Marx, and Michael Bakunin—vied for a following on the continent of Europe. By 1888 Marx's materialistic approach dominated the growing socialist revolution as laborers accepted the *Communist Manifesto* as their common platform. Familiar with the three schools of thought, Scudder thought that Mazzini's idealism and unrealistic appeals to a higher sense of morality prevented him from securing a lasting following of his own. In her article on "Socialism and Sacrifice" she described Mazzini:

> We are dealing with a glorious nature in unstable equilibrium: treading too often not on the terra firma of the actual but a tight-rope gossamer spun spider-like from within. Here is a great man; here is no founder of a great or living school.[9]

Attracted to the practicality of Marx's and Bakunin's solutions to the social problem, Scudder somewhat reluctantly endorsed the Marxist doctrine of economic determinism.

From Marx's statement she learned that "the advance of economic forces has always been, and is still, the determining base of all advance, religious, philosophic, political, and social."[10] Experience had proved to her that in each social organization the ruling class determined the form of government, set the moral standards, and exercised all forms of social control. A brutally honest statement from *Socialism and Character* provided an example of the cruel social reality that Scudder encountered by befriending the working class.

> Take the working girl, for example, and gather up in imagination the total effect of all the benevolent agencies which exist to help her: the girls' club, the settlement, the vacation house, the Associated Charities, if worst comes to worst, and even the Woman's trade-union League. Measure the force of their reaction on her personality in comparison with that of two crude economic facts—the wage she receives and the duration of her working day. The worth of our eager efforts dwindles both comically and tragically in our eyes, and the broad economic condition bulks out of all proportion as the real master of that woman's life.[11]

Not even philanthropic impulses or charity could break the chains of economic necessity that imprisoned the young girl Scudder described.

One may question why Scudder did not utterly disconnect herself from Marx's materialistic interpretation of history. She thought that Marx's views could lend support to her religious conception of history. They provided something more vital to hold human beings together than purely moral ideals.[12] The doctrine of economic determinism taught that "those moral forces which, from sweep and mass, count the most in progress, are not generated apart from life, in the heart or conscience of the exceptional individual, but out of the very conditions of life itself."[13] Citizens did not enjoy unlimited, free power to control their own social progress; economic forces, in large measure, determined their advance. Scudder believed that the doctrine of determinism clarified social thought by helping reformers to avoid "a depressing waste of effort."[14] Rightly applied, the notion of determinism ensured that reformers would not base ideals for social change on moral abstractions but root them in the soil of the economic realities that confronted her generation.

Scudder accepted the doctrine of class consciousness with greater enthusiasm than its sister doctrine even though she knew that her support of it welcomed discontent. Georg Lukács pointed out that Marx never clearly defined the term *class consciousness*.[15] The omission of a concise definition from Marx's work facilitated the development of various interpretations of this doctrine. Scudder interpreted the term to mean that society was divided into classes along the lines of the contribution an individual makes to the means of production. Many religious thinkers dismissed the idea of class consciousness because it was associated with political militancy, as evidenced in the strikes, boycotts, and lockouts that were growing at a staggering rate. Scudder, however, did not see fear of militant attitudes as reason enough to dismiss the doctrine. She argued that awareness of class divisions unmasked loyalties given to class at the expense of the common good; it gave voice to groups of people who had been silenced, and it had the power to widen sympathies for the working classes.

Furthermore, class consciousness served as encouragement to working-class people to clarify ways to address and solve their own problems. The upper classes were not going to secure the social and financial security of hired laborers.[16] In *Socialism and Character* Scudder endorsed teaching about the divisions among classes to enliven "that imaginative power which democracy most needs."[17] The working classes did not seek "the transfer of privilege, but the abolition of privilege; and while they work for the emancipation of their own class, they believe not only that this class comprises the majority of mankind, but [also] that its freedom will enable all men to breath a more liberal air."[18]

Scudder's religious beliefs provided the real basis for faith in class consciousness. Confidence in class consciousness came from God's confidence in humanity. Splintering the human community into classes based on their wealth and prestige was material, divisive, and unholy.[19] Plain people carried a reverence for the physical needs of all and recognized the value of each person's contribution to the social body. Movements toward class consciousness raised awareness about the deeper sacramental sanctity pervading all human life. The more cooperative order advocated by the working class promised to translate "what life offers into a higher likeness."[20] It seemed that trends toward socialism were leading modern society toward the social body that God had prepared for it.[21]

Not limiting the term *class consciousness* to the working class, Scudder hoped that a group consciousness would develop with the potential to create a bond among people in every nation. She attributed two positive results to the growing awareness among the classes: inner discipline among the working class and widening social sympathies.[22] In the end, Scudder valued the doctrine because she believed that by uncovering social biases class consciousness ultimately moved society toward greater loyalty to the whole.

Socialism: "A Stream Nearing a Waterfall"

The spread of socialism in Europe and the United States was a sign to Scudder that people were impatient for social change. Evidence of widespread interest in socialist policies served as a resource for her understanding of the current social circumstances. She saw the establishment of socialism as the most important intellectual event of the late nineteenth century. Socialism challenged the premise upon which people had built several of the world's greatest democratic governments: the principle that private property was a sacred and inalienable right. Scudder recognized that the Declaration of Rights in France used the American Declaration of Independence as its model. "The Constitution of 1793 in its second article defined the rights of man as 'Equality, Liberty, Security, and Property,' and it was not less a man than Danton who said at the first sitting of the Convention, 'Let us declare that all properties, territorial, individual and industrial, shall be forever respected.'"[23] With the rise of socialism the principle that private property was a right held to be sacred became less an assumption than a thesis to be proved.

Socialism reached the height of its influence in America between the years 1897 and 1912. After the party had won the support of one-third of the American Federation of Labor and organized an international network of industrial workers, it claimed over 150 thousand dues-paying members. Hundreds of newspapers circulated socialist ideas. In 1912, Eugene Debs won nearly one million votes for his candidacy for the U.S. presidency. Socialists had also made significant inroads in Congress by securing the passage of a considerable body of legislation.[24] Just three years before Scudder published *Socialism and Character*, she characterized the socialist movement as a stream nearing a waterfall.

> With the socialist party in Germany gaining a million votes in five years; with a socialist labour-party represented in the British Parliament; with the Pan-Anglican Congress drawing its largest and most eager audiences to hear socialism discussed and in the main endorsed by the clergy, indications thicken. In Latin Europe the socialists are a force to be increasingly reckoned with: if the movement in America is less concentrated than in smaller or more autocratic countries, the sentiment is perhaps more widely diffused. . . . The stream is broad, and we have not shot Niagara yet; but the sound we hear may be the roar of the approaching falls.[25]

With the politics of the world in flux, the conditions were ripe for social change. In the years following World War One, Scudder and her dear friend and companion began to say this prayer before meals: "We have food: others have none: God bless the revolution!"[26] But most Christians, particularly Catholics, approached socialist ideas with a large degree of skepticism. Many socialists were equally suspicious of Christian groups and saw organized religion as harmful to the working class.

One could find some Social Gospel leaders among the ranks of those skeptical about socialist policies, and they remained hesitant to make an unfettered commitment to the Socialist Party. The socialist doctrines of economic determinism and class consciousness prevented Jane Addams from joining the party. Immigrants' living conditions in Chicago taught Addams that one's social environment strongly impacted the shaping of human nature. On this point she agreed with socialists. What she could not assent to, however, was their "crude interpretation of the class conflict."[27] Though she longed for a satisfactory explanation of social chaos, she found the doctrines of economic determinism and class consciousness inadequate. Lecturing in both urban and rural communities, Addams noticed that Americans living in rural areas were unaware of class disputes. Hence, it was not right to read "human documents" through a single lens. She wrote that she "should have been glad to have had the comradeship of the gallant company [of socialists] had they not firmly insisted that fellowship depends on identity of a creed."[28] Scudder thought that Addams needed to look at the doctrines more closely. In response to Addams's concerns, Scudder commented that idealists might be legitimately inclined to repel the crass presentation of these doctrines by earlier socialists, but "when looked at closely, economic determinism at least is a very innocent bogey."[29]

Ely and Rauschenbusch never joined the Socialist Party but were sympathetic with socialist views. Neither Ely nor Rauschenbusch could agree with socialists regarding the extent to which public policies should be socialized, but both maintained the belief that some degree of socialization would increase justice. Accused by Oliver Wells of being a socialist, Ely defended himself in an article published in *The Forum* in 1894. He endorsed the socialization of natural monopolies but identified several "insuperable difficulties" with socialism. Rauschenbusch considered himself a socialist but refused to join the party. Scudder hoped that he would make the commitment. In 1912 she offered him some encouragement: "I covet you for the party!" she wrote. "My being in it doesn't count except to myself. Yours would. It would draw many and we could get a political socialism, of a better type."[30]

The Socialist Party, however, did cultivate relationships with some Christian leaders and secured their membership in the party and their advocacy on behalf of socialist agendas. Scudder was not alone among Christian Socialists who aimed to persuade other religious believers to accept a joint venture between socialism and Christianity. Christian leaders committed to the Socialist Party agreed that Christianity inspired their membership. Capitalism was a negative force that impeded the spiritual growth of the religious and the evolution of Christian democratic ideals; however, social change informed by Christian beliefs promised the inward transformation necessary for true democracy to be realized. In his essay "The Negro and Socialism," Reverdy Ransom asserted:

> Socialism, like the inspired Carpenter of Nazareth, places more value upon man than it does upon riches. It believes that the rights of man are more sacred than the rights of property, believes indeed, that the only sacred thing on earth is a human being. Socialism would bring all the people to participate in the rivalry of life upon a footing of equality, allowing to each individual the widest possible range for the development of his powers and personality, with freedom to follow wherever his abilities may lead him.[31]

Scudder's Experience of Working-Class Life

For Scudder, experience had tested and proved socialist creeds. Every city in the United States could produce evidence to support her assertions. In *Yankee Reformers in an Urban Age*, Arthur Mann reported that the divisions evident in Boston were typical of American cities between 1890 and 1900. Communities distinguished themselves by the type of people living within their bounds. Class and race separated people into different enclaves.

People recognized the Back Bay district for its prestige and Victorian flair, whereas the North End had a reputation for its tenements and the human riffraff cluttering its streets. By 1900 more than twenty-five nationalities made the North End their home. The working class primarily lived in the city's dreary South End.[32] Factors of class and economics determined where and how well people lived.

Scudder lived in fashionable sections of Boston and came from a privileged family, but she never grew callous or indifferent to the needs of others. Work in the settlement movement, involvement in labor strikes, and her advocacy for women introduced Scudder to the economic and spiritual disparities created by the industrial order. As a strong proponent and worker in the settlement movement, Scudder found settlements' greatest influence "less in their achievement of results than in their revelation of conditions."[33] Remembering the surroundings of a settlement on St. Mary's Street in Philadelphia, Scudder wrote:

> The people around are very poor. Indeed, one learns what poverty means for the first time in living among them through the bitter winter weather. They live huddled together, whole families sometimes with lodgers thrown in occupying a single room; they have few clothes to wear, little fuel, often nothing particular to eat for days at a time, seldom steady work. They belong to the "left-overs," the submerged tenth.[34]

Industrial society had turned up its nose at the "idle poor" for their lack of productivity. Many of Boston's poor had recently emigrated from Europe. A wave of immigrants flowed into the city from the middle to late nineteenth century. Economics determined their value to Boston society. Factors that facilitated their need to emigrate influenced their ability to carve a niche for themselves in the United States. Skilled laborers assimilated more easily and resumed familiar work routines. Unskilled laborers, mostly peasants transplanted into an urban commercial center, lacked the training and capital to make a smooth transition.[35] They did not enjoy job security and often lost their jobs. This situation was not unique to the Boston area. Scudder described the situation of a family in Philadelphia: "Mr. Meadow will work—if he can find a job. He is not skilled; no one ever taught him anything. . . . Has the world no place for him?[36]

Barriers raised by economic discrimination were not the only dividers between Boston's poor and well-to-do. With their attitudes toward poverty, high society snubbed the underclasses. They expected the poor to suffer. A conversation between two characters in *A Listener in Babel* was particularly instructive about prevalent attitudes toward the poor:

> "You can't expect the shiftless not to suffer," Miss Harding went on. "Why shouldn't they suffer?"
>
> "They should," Janet retorted, "if right to live is measured by service rendered the community."[37]

The callous disregard the rich held for the poor angered Scudder. A reporter quoted her saying that she "felt like blowing up Commonwealth Avenue with a bomb in order to arouse its unsympathetic inhabitants to the needs of the poor about them."[38]

Scudder found it nonsensical that society condemned the "idle" poor while idolizing the life of what she called the "idle" rich. Why celebrate the achievements of those "pleasure-lovers" who sat on their duffs while living off the profits made by common laborers? She pointed out that neither contributed to society anything deemed productive. In Janet's words, "I wish we applied [the principle] to the shiftless rich as well as to the shiftless poor."[39]

The working-class folks found themselves sandwiched between the rich and the destitute. As an advocate of the labor movement, Scudder sympathetically listened to the stories told by ill-treated factory hands and clerks. In 1912 textile workers in Lawrence invited Scudder and her Wellesley colleague, Ellen Hayes, to visit with them. Recalling her experience of Lawrence, Scudder said, "I visited the workers' homes, bad enough to justify almost any revolt in my indignant eyes."[40] Though her contact with the strike was minimal, she addressed a meeting called by a women's committee regarding problems developing out of the strike. Strikers had planned to send their hungry children to safe havens provided by sympathizers in Philadelphia. Police informed by the manufacturers prevented the departure of the children and beat the women that accompanied them. Some severely criticized Scudder for her involvement in the Lawrence Striker's Meeting because they thought leaders had held the meeting under the auspices of the Industrial Workers of the World. Some even asked that Wellesley's trustees demand her resignation. In defense of her actions, Scudder in *The Boston Common* published the speech that she gave at the striker's meeting.[41] Her speech showed her outrage at the factory's mistreatment of women and children. Through her alliance with the women, she identified herself as an advocate for their cause.

No one felt society's imperviousness more acutely than women. Lack of government regulation for the working conditions of women and children gave factories permission to take advantage of them. Rauschenbusch shared Scudder's sense of indignation for women whom the factories were mistreating. In *Christianizing the Social Order* he remembered the story of a young girl who was concerned about her safety. She reported to her manager that if she continued to operate the machine assigned to her, it would cut off her arm. He gruffly responded that he did not pay her to make such judgments. Her worst fears were realized. After the machine severed her arm and disabled her, she sued the factory so that she would have an income. The factory, however, won the court battle because she admitted that she knew about the danger involved in operating the machinery and therefore continued working at her own risk.[42]

Scudder judged society guilty of handicapping "all but the very few born to privilege of wealth or capacity, and at the same time it had thrown on every individual the onus of creating his own place in the economic scheme."[43] Society left the poor, those who had little or no economic value to the production of industry, to satisfy their own needs. Working-class folk subsisted on meager wages and worked at the mercy of the factory owners. Again speaking through the voice of Janet Frothingham, Scudder conveyed a sense of urgency about the need for social change:

> Our industrial system doesn't starve people outright, you know. It keeps them constantly underfed and anxious, but with just enough hope so that their enfeebled bodies and minds shrink from change, lest a worse thing befall them.[44]

The hardscrabble lives of tenement dwellers were shocking, but their material suffering was not the only impoverishment that disturbed Scudder. Thomas Carlyle's words had captured her attention: "That there should one man die ignorant who had capacity for knowledge, this I call a tragedy, should it happen twenty times to the minute, as by some computations it does."[45] These people knew intellectual and spiritual deprivation, not just material poverty. Settlements also aimed to meet the spiritual and intellectual needs of their constituents. Denison House in Boston's North End put a dent in the trade of saloon keepers and local pool rooms by offering programs aimed at providing intellectual stimulation for the unprivileged of Boston. Hull House in Chicago sponsored visiting lecturers to speak about the newest ideas in social reform. Prominent guests included Rauschenbusch and the colorful George Herron. Scudder recognized that the settlements acted as effective agencies to expand the intellectual horizons of the poor and as centers for new thought.

Ultimately, however, Scudder thought settlements were unable to attain the kind of community for which she hoped. Their popularity attested to the awakening of the nation's moral conscience; by 1900 there were over two hundred settlement houses in the United States,[46] but they were largely supported by the upper classes. Unfortunately, settlement workers were often unable to comfortably move out of their accepted social roles to see the working class as their equals. Providing a place in which the wealthy encountered the working poor was not enough; society's attitudes toward poverty and orientation toward charity had to be transformed.

An Ethics of Inequality

In *Socialism and Character*, Scudder argued that economic inequality bred an "ethics of inequality."[47] Each social class had an ethic based upon its privilege or lack of it. After examining both "the ethics of privilege" and "the ethics of want," Scudder concluded that both fell far short of inspiring the kind of loving community known in God.

Relying on what Scudder called the "chivalry of those who have," an ethic of privilege assumed the responsibility of the upper classes to assist those beneath them. Modern charity required social superiority. Scudder assessed the ethics of privilege as an old, casual, uncritical understanding of generosity that was demoralizing and inadequate. "Its day is past, with that of machicolated battlements and Byzantine mosaics."[48] Modern charity as chivalry was not good for the poor or the rich. Philanthropists often acted out of the wrong motives. Scudder described the system as "those vast benevolences of modern life which are too often ostentatious returns from secret cruelties."[49]

Scudder made her views regarding philanthropic interests extremely clear when she placed her teaching position in jeopardy by leading a group of faculty members in protesting a gift the Standard Oil Company offered to Wellesley College in 1900.[50] At the time Wellesley College needed financial support, but Scudder argued that the college should shrink from the opportunity to accept "tainted money." She appealed to Caroline Hazard, president of Wellesley, and the board of trustees not to accept the money. After checking with economists, Hazard wrote to Scudder that they had assured her that the money was "good."[51] The college accepted the gift. Scudder questioned whether or not she should resign but felt that she and other faculty members had already done enough to alienate members of the board.

Some philanthropists experimented with more democratic attendance to charity. Scudder cited the Salvation Army as an example.[52] The Salvation Army displayed a real sensitivity and interest in the poor, but when compared to a cooperative vision for society, they still missed the mark. Even with a greater consciousness of democratic ideals, their work and the work of other philanthropists was unsuccessful. To help bring a truly democratic order, charity needed to be redefined. Real democracy snuffed out a brand of charity that assumed the superiority of one class over another. Scudder suggested that the modern situation called for systemic changes that would engender authentic justice and mercy.

At the other end of the ethical spectrum lay the morals of modern poverty. Social conditions required the poor to act with humility and to sacrifice for the sake of others. Involuntary renunciation of goods was their way of life. Though the poor were in a "much safer moral condition today than the rich,"[53] the ethics of want also prevented them from living up to the ideals taught by Jesus. The poverty known by tenement dwellers was not the voluntary renunciation of goods glorified in the New Testament and medieval records. Instead, Scudder characterized impoverished people as "reluctant victims . . . dragged along the weary flats of life, entangled in . . . [their] bonds."[54] Industry held the lower classes in bondage and prevented the poor from seeking a life of love and detachment from the world. Two of the ideals that Jesus conveyed in his Sermon on the Mount remained "a forbidden luxury to the self-respecting poor."[55]

Scudder's assessment of the social situation was clear: competition in industrial society undercut a Christian conception of democracy, created the conditions for widespread social stratification, encouraged an ethic dictated by one's social standing, and threatened the moral health of all citizens. She believed that realizing God's vision of a cooperative society had become a moral dilemma for Americans. She and others were aware of the larger Christian vision for society but could scarcely move themselves beyond the myopic outlook of competitive society. Clearly, the individualism encouraged by competition promoted character flaws. After deeming the moral progress of the nation as "progressively rotten,"[56] Scudder judged an ethics of inequality unsatisfactory. For stronger character to evolve, society had to be reshaped.

Creating a Better Moral Environment

By changing the environment itself, Scudder thought it possible, even highly probable, to alter the egregious effects that the social environment was having on character. She pushed for moderns to allow themselves to be shaped by another hand:

> Let the Potter's Wheel, as the ages pass, twirl faster; let it mold the clay into forms increasingly complex, by pressure increasingly heavy, involved, and severe. If the vessel emerge in greater and more serviceable beauty, the gain is clear; and the clay will sing to the pressure of the wheel.[57]

Scudder thought that socialist policies had the greatest potential to enable society to operate more in accordance with God's natural law and to more closely approximate God's vision for a new heaven and a new earth. When she speculated about the moral improvements that society would make if it were to realize the Cooperative Commonwealth, Scudder's conception was sometimes difficult to visualize; however, she did offer a broad outline of the attitudes, behaviors, and practices that needed to evolve in order to create an environment that would nurture stronger moral character. A more cooperative social order would reward individual holiness rather than individual sin. Citizens would think of freedom in terms of shared power and make decisions with the interest of the larger community in mind. Scudder did not intend for anyone to think of the Cooperative Commonwealth as a permanent solution for the world's problems. At that time, socialist policies offered the most promise to address the complex global situation.

Freedom, Power, and Shaping Moral Character

To take initial steps toward creating an environment out of which stronger moral character might evolve, individuals needed to begin to see their relationship to a larger social whole. Freedom and power emerged as key elements in Scudder's discussion of an environment that would facilitate individual allegiance to the broader community. Scudder thought that people should consider freedom as a "term of social rather than individual import, never to be realized by the one while the many are still bound."[58] Freedom related to all members of the human race and God's vision for the community. Scudder picked up on a theme also central to discussions held by socialists and capitalists, but took a different approach. Socialists advocated the use of freedom to increase power for the good of the commoners. Capitalists interpreted freedom as the removal of restrictions to increase the power of an individual to affect a free-market economy. Scudder emphasized humans' freedom to shape their environment so that they could mirror Divine Society, thereby increasing the common good:

> True liberty is positive, not negative, dealing less with the removal of restriction than with the imparting of power. It consists not in the licence of each person to indulge desire, but in the power bestowed by the community upon its every member to rise to the level of his richest capacity by living in harmony with the Whole.[59]

She hoped that society would draw upon God's love to fashion itself in God's cooperative image. Ultimately, the only way to freedom was through the voluntary renunciation of one's material possessions and the sense of individual rights associated with them.

Before the Russian revolution, Scudder directed her attention toward Marx's materialistic interpretation of history. Friedrich Engels explained that Marx exposed history as an account of class struggles or "contests between exploiting and exploited, ruling and ruled classes."[60] Communists worldwide rallied to fight against oppression by bringing the question of private ownership of property to the forefront everywhere. The solution to the property question was to promote group ownership of property. They would increase power among the lower classes by transferring the ownership of property. Although Scudder thought this was not a bad idea in itself, she nonetheless questioned the foundation upon which Marxists built their vision for society.

From Scudder's perspective, idealists placed too great an emphasis on their materialistic interpretation of history and disregarded God's interest in human affairs. This mistake, Scudder warned, would prove to be fatal for socialists:

> The militant socialists are too busily engaged in aggressive propaganda: so preoccupied with *their vision* of healing and liberation for the body that they lay themselves open to the charge of feeling slight interest in the soul. The conservatives are absorbed in defence. Yet in the confusion one fact is clear: should socialism come otherwise than as the result of an inward transformation, affecting the deep springs of will and love, it would prove the worst disaster of any experiment in collective living that the world has seen.[61]

Marxists, she charged, had mistakenly based their higher moral ideal on human inventiveness. They "were convinced that it was incumbent on them to invent the right plan for managing the universe."[62]

Capitalistic society, on the other hand, supported laws that emphasize the freedom of the individual. A free market motivated ambition through economic incentives. Capitalists considered the market to be "impersonal" and separated economics from political views. With their purchasing power, individuals had the freedom to represent themselves in the market. The emphasis here was on removal of restrictions to promote individual freedom. For example, David Ricardo thought that competition rewarded innovation and provided the opportunity for individual advancement. He criticized laws used to restrict the competition, such as wage laws: "Like all other contracts, wages should be left to the fair and free competition of the market."[63] The market defined the value of the individual's contribution and was represented as morally neutral. Scudder saw no moral neutrality in the free-market economy.

She agreed with socialists' and capitalists' emphasis on freedom and power as defining factors in the social environment. Capitalists' aims were to maintain power for individuals. Marx and many socialists promoted a kind of power swap by increasing power for the underclasses. Operating on assumptions more familiar to Mazzini, Scudder argued that human beings were free to assume the power to affect social change but needed to draw upon God's vision for it. Capitalists and many idealists failed to account for the real force that funds morality:

> Moral forces, like physical, are out of our power to create, and refusal to recognize our helplessness is responsible for our chief blunders. But, like the physical, they are within our power to control, direct, and transform: and in this fact lies the justification for that hesitant instinct which, when it confronts scientific determinism in the sociological sphere, feels more strongly impelled than ever before to stress the reality of freedom. Man's function on this planet is not to make, but to reshape.[64]

One does not find true freedom in the freedom to fashion one's own destiny. Seeking freedom in community and solidarity in freedom[65] brings real freedom. Socialists had the right idea that shared property creates the conditions for freedom, but the socialist vision in the end had to reflect Divine Society. God's love is the real creative force driving social trends that move toward greater equality.

In its most positive sense, freedom imparts shared power. "It consists, not in the license of each person to indulge desire, but in the power bestowed by the community upon its every member to rise to the level of his richest capacity by living in harmony with the Whole."[66] The importance of ingenuity lay not in human ability to fashion a world in its own likeness, but rather in the privilege to cooperate with a greater "Will" revealed in the changing order.

According to Scudder, the international surge of interest in socialism before World War One marked an opportunity in history where moral and "natural" forces had the opportunity to work together. Socialism born of an inward transformation required the voluntary renunciation of personal rights in order to allocate power for the common good. Making an allusion to Jesus' voluntary sacrifice as the test of true freedom, Scudder wrote: "The only thorough proof of freedom has always been a willing submission; and the capacity for living in harmony with the whole may again and again prove a kenosis or self-emptying."[67] Standing at another "historic juncture," society could now choose to live into a higher likeness. Aided by a spiritual dimension, socialism had the potential to reshape society in its intended, cooperative image.

The rapidly changing social context that Scudder confronted continually challenged her thoughts about freedom and power. New political developments gave her the opportunity to take account of her position and strengthen her arguments. Until World War One, Scudder felt quite optimistic about humans' ability to grab hold of their own social destinies: "Human nature alters perpetually, before our very eyes. The stuff is malleable, nay, fluid, and its changes are the soul of progress."[68] History had identified certain heroes who had acted out of a deeper moral purpose rather than as agents for personal gain. Figures like Lincoln had achieved great things because things had been "done through and not by them."[69] They did not impose their own personal views upon the world, but worked to bring society closer in line with God's vision for it. As the rhythm beating at the heart of the universe, God's love made the evolution of a society in God's image inevitable.

> Determinism, then, simply puts civilization under that reign of law which it is always open to us to construe as the reign of love. It assures us that the threads of moral purpose are knit into the woof of the universe instead of trailing vacuously through space.[70]

Though Scudder consistently focused on the right motivation behind the pursuit of freedom, before the Russian revolution she advocated radical means to achieve shared power. In 1917, she justified the use of violence to bring about peace and freedom for those suffering from social injustice.[71] However, problems caused by the communism that developed in Russia and other parts of the world moved Scudder to shift her focus from Marx's revolutionary ideas and to look more closely at Christian visionaries. The social change brought about by force had created more problems for the Soviets than solutions to the challenges of poverty that they faced.

When considering the situation in postwar Russia, Scudder concluded that coercion did not really change the social order. The Russian revolution never brought with it real freedom. She then with greater intentionality began studying Franciscan communities. Spiritually charged by their profound dependence on God, the first Franciscans had voluntarily renounced their worldly goods and attained real "freedom, joy and power."[72] The desire of individuals to change must bring about social change. They cannot attain real freedom by the use of force.

After retiring from Wellesley, Scudder mulled over her older ideas. She admitted in *On Journey* that her thoughts presented in *Socialism and Character* never changed significantly. Her later writings, however, show a better understanding of the complexity of the political environment and a stronger emphasis upon Franciscanism. On the surface it appears that this shift in her thinking may be a retreat from earlier ideas, but in making this change Scudder actually becomes more consistent. She begins to recognize war as an extreme form of social competition.

Furthering her earlier discussions of freedom, she wrote that she was "surer and surer that freedom is a discipline rather than a privilege."[73] She did not think of freedom as a good in itself but only as a means and a condition of the good. Two world wars, economic sanctions against Germany, the climate of discrimination in the United States, and communism translated as totalitarianism in Russia—all these conditioned Scudder's attitude. Complementing her earlier work, she compared the human experience of freedom to autumn leaves falling from a tree and minimized the value of unrestricted freedom.

> Silently the gold leaves detached themselves, and with soft erratic waverings floated down to the waiting earth. I watched them find that freedom toward which they had always strained, tugging at their restraining twigs whenever breezes blew. Liberty theirs at last—but liberty to die. For living freedom is that of the leaf tight fastened, with the sap of the tree of which it is a product and a part vibrating through it, controlling it, till it reaches its mature being, its perfect form.[74]

Unrestricted freedoms were a "devastating nuisance."[75] Where society granted more freedom to some individuals, it took freedom away from others. Worthwhile freedom sprouts from a deeper root. "Liberty," Scudder surmised, "must be scrutinized in the light of the end to be gained by it; . . . its ultimate worth . . . [is] not in escape from restraint but in power bestowed for self-realization."[76] Freedom requires disciplining oneself to surrender privileges for the good of all.

Scudder's Vision of the Cooperative Commonwealth

Trying to lure religious skeptics to support socialism, Scudder presented a vision for a more just society in *Socialism and Character*. For her, the highest reason to work for social change was the desire to liberate the religious life. Socialism informed by Christianity required discipline and would impact character by inviting individuals to renounce their personal rights voluntarily for the common good. Socialism would make some specific achievements: Justice for all would replace rule by self-interest. Human beings, not profits, would be the end of production. The collective rather than individuals would make decisions regarding compensation for work. Laws of religious ethics would become the fundamental laws of social health and ultimately lead society toward "Real" freedom.

Individuals would no longer determine their own relationship to justice. Replacing the "free fierce conflict between self-interest and love,"[77] justice for all would be the informing principle of the Cooperative Commonwealth. God's "predetermined rhythm" would pervade all social relations and allow the "highest opportunities of Love."[78] Clearly, Scudder linked the terms "justice" and "love" to God's nature as a social being who modeled a Divine Society based upon equality and love. Social justice was connected not only to material goods, but also to spiritual justice. The highest opportunity of love was to clear a pathway for all people to gain equal access to God's love and to live freely in that love.

Capitalism assessed the value of individuals in society according to their ability to contribute to production, but socialism would reassess their value. In a competitive environment, those with strong character could manipulate a good end to their social destinies by creating a place for themselves in the world of industry. Wealth seemed to be the test of character. In a socialist state, people would no longer measure one's contribution to society according to monetary gain. By shifting the center of consciousness from a monetary reward to the process of production and its result upon character, socialism changed the value of individual contributions to society. The measure of one's contribution would be "to gain from him the largest product compatible with his well-being of mind and body."[79] The test of character would become less in creation than in the use of conditions.

Accepting socialism did not necessarily imply uniform compensation. Scudder agreed with capitalists that workers should receive differentiated pay. In the Cooperative Commonwealth, remuneration would vary according to the personal factor and social cost. A worker would receive "what he needs to keep him at this point."[80] Those who wanted to work harder could receive more than their allotted quota. She differed, however, in her understanding of who should decide how society would distribute the reward for work. The entire community, not individuals, should bear the responsibility to measure the reward for work. Collective decisions and democratic control, not individuals, should carry decisions regarding the compensation of workers.

This was not a vision of a perfect "Fra Angelico paradise."[81] The Cooperative Commonwealth would help society move toward a closer approximation of the kingdom of God but was not synonymous with it. The new society would not eliminate suffering. Rather, socialism would create the conditions that were more likely to guard against self-contempt and self-conceit. Social reform would come with average people in mind—weary laborers, children presently resigned to industrial slavery, and women sick with worry as they wondered where they would find food for the next family meal. Individuals would voluntarily choose to limit themselves, which meant less social waste and more for these others. Scudder's hope was that society would opt to move along in harmony with God's natural rhythm, free itself from the tyranny of economic fear, and cease its idolatry of the god of greed.

The Ethics of Equality

Scudder predicted the moral yield of a socialist state: whereas social inequality bred an ethic of inequality and fostered "aristocratic virtues that stoop,"[82] the Cooperative Commonwealth would give room for an ethics of equality to grow. A new social order would reinterpret the value of charity, compassion, and sympathy and nurture these virtues from the "lowlands." If motivated by an inward transformation, moderns could "look forward to equality of opportunity in ethics as well as economics."[83] Class divisions would no longer dictate modern morality; instead, all attitudes—of those living in poverty or in privilege—would be common heritage. Keeping in mind that Divine Society was the model for social equality, principles Jesus taught in his Sermon on the Mount were to inform the ethics of equality. The egalitarian ethic evident in socialist ideologies would allow society to bring itself back into harmony with the rhythm of God's love that infuses the universe.

An ethics of inequality defined charity as a responsibility of the rich toward the poor and encouraged class division. Scudder argued that Paul linked *charis* to a way of life rather than to monetary gifts. The fact that society first opted for money doles when charity was mentioned supported Scudder's conclusion that society had failed to understand what Paul meant. Taking a cue from Paul, the Cooperative Commonwealth would separate charity from monetary giving. Christ's own sacrifice would illumine charity and interpret it as a spiritual atmosphere rather than an activity exerted by the wealthy on behalf of the poor.

A dim shadow of real compassion, modern charity too often defined compassion in terms of pity for the less fortunate. Christ called for compassion understood as spiritual generosity: "We shall be no longer haunted in summer by the aching consciousness of the poor in great cities, of the thronged factories, the dying sick, the languishing children," Scudder wrote. But the new social order would relieve society from "intolerable pity."[84]

Scudder observed that "sympathy" was the Greek form of the Latin term for compassion. According to Scudder, sympathy was the "chief psychic force leading us toward the socialist state."[85] As the "keystone" virtue of socialism, sympathy enabled human beings to feel the pain of others and grieve with them. Practicing sympathy meant transforming one's way of life. In Scudder's words, "Each detail of daily behavior could be transformed from a triumph of bargaining to a sacrament of service."[86] Focusing one's energy on the virtue of sympathy gave endless opportunities to be more generous and affectionate toward others.

Scudder reinterpreted the virtues of charity, compassion, and sympathy in light of Pauline texts and Jesus' teachings: "The source and archetype of the whole movement which we sum up in the formula, the 'return to nature,' is to be found in the Sermon on the Mount."[87] Jesus' sermon invited society to put the poor, meek, and humble first. She aimed to open up to everyone virtues that in her context the poor chiefly fostered. Viewing the world from the perspective of the underclasses meant to understand the need for egalitarianism and the desire to restore the social order to the natural rhythm of the universe: "It is for us to imitate the life of Nature, not her death, and that life is fulfilled not in antagonisms but in reciprocity of ordered service."[88]

The Church and the Cooperative Commonwealth

Scudder did not expect an orderly, easy transition to a socialist state. She was well aware that the transition would not benefit all in the same way. With humor characteristic of her writings, she compared her contemporaries to children throwing temper tantrums when threatened by rules imposed upon them by their nannies. "Distaste for discipline is innate in the human breast. We all wail in unison with the little boy in *Peter Pan*, who cries, 'I don't want to take my bath!' as good Nana trots him sternly to the tub."[89] Surprisingly, it was not the most ardent social agitators who would weather the change without pain. Scudder saw them as too invested in their own self-interests. Neither would the wealthiest classes fare well through the transition. Those who would fare best through the transition were those inwardly prepared for the new order.

> Who can doubt that it will be he who has trained himself spiritually for the new order—who by watchful self-control has developed the new social intuitions, the swift perception of that delicate point where the pressure of his own claim and powers might inflict injury rather than help on others? This is the man who will make the inner strength of the new state; and it is he who will rejoice in the new order.[90]

Therefore, the Church as the mother of faith and the teacher of equality had a special charge and investment in addressing the social situation.

Borrowing Thomas Carlyle's words, Scudder confirmed that the world had invited the Church to help solve the social problem: "The world asks of its Church in these times more passionately than of any other institution, 'Canst thou teach us or not?'"[91] The mission of the modern Church was to regain its collective life and the excitement of its earliest years. Mimicking the first Pentecostal experience, the Church could again illumine the world about the stirring of the Spirit of equality. She admitted that the Church was a victim of social stratification, but it also remained a unique institution based upon Christian doctrine and infused by the Spirit. Unlike approaches to social change rooted in humanism, the Church worked toward a "human race, made in the image of God."[92] The Church had the potential to raise a distinctive voice in the struggle for industrial democracy.

The Church and the Ethics of Inequality

Like many other Social Gospelers, Scudder recognized the Church's tendency to behave like any other corporate body. In recent years the Church neglected the social aspect of its mission, benefited from the wealth and property placed at its disposal, and allowed the middle class to dominate its membership rosters. The Church often reflected the same ethics of inequality fostered by society.

In concert with figures like Ely and Rauschenbusch, she believed that the Church failed to live out its mission to alleviate distress in society. In *The Social Aspects of Christianity* Ely charged that the Church had neglected the social aspect of its mission. What had the Church done with the second commandment, "Love your neighbor as yourself"? Relying on her reading of Christian history, Scudder declared that "to draw out the social significance of the Gospels, to define Christian duty in terms of industrial justice for an industrial age, was a task wholly neglected and desperately necessary."[93] Like Ely, Scudder thought that the Church failed to recognize Jesus' double commission. The Church had inherited a type of piety from the last century that was

> suave-mannered, pleasant-voiced; endangering nothing in particular, an ornament to the Sunday pews; devoted to good causes in proportion to their remoteness, . . . but so far as home affairs are concerned, ignorant alike to the ardors of the mystic and the heroisms of the reformers.[94]

Of the two types of Christianity that had become influential, social Christianity and spiritual Christianity, the Church opted to emphasize the latter by focusing on the importance of inward salvation and neglecting its partnership with outward action.

Making similar charges against the Church, Rauschenbusch in *Christianity and the Social Crisis* called attention to the economic ramifications of the Church's choices. He described the Church as a victim of social stratification. The middle class was the best source of income for the Church and supplied the greatest number of its constituents. Churches owned property in the same fashion as businesses or individuals. The Church had a smaller supply of ministers because it depended upon the presupposition of financial equality among members as well as volunteers. In other words, the modern Church operated according to worldly values.[95]

In addition, the composition of the Church reflected the ordering evident in society. Working-class persons were noticeably absent from the pews. The voluntary basis of the Church in America made it an organization dependent upon the privileged classes for support.[96] Working-class people had no forum in which they could voice their opinions. In "How Draw Workingmen to Church?" Scudder quoted the statement of a social worker that exposed the seriousness of the problem:

> I've been to thronged down-town Churches where there was admirable and spiritual preaching. But I never yet saw the kind of people there that I see in a Trade-Union meeting. I never see them in ANY Church.[97]

The Church and the Ethics of Equality

Scudder called for Christian communities to focus more intentionally on modeling an ethic of equality. Although she acknowledged the failures of the Church, Scudder viewed it as an entity unlike any other institution. Of all the forces at work in society, the Church was society's best hope for achieving a cooperative order. Humanist approaches could not achieve the kind of real social transformation needed. The Church, however, had a special charge to equip its members to help society move toward the type of cooperation understood in the model of the Trinity. By reinterpreting their doctrines, Christians could draw upon the Church's rich store of wisdom to address ever-changing and often problematic social realities:

> If we could show a clear relation between belief in the Blessed Trinity and right social policies or attitudes, we should go far forward to decide whether that belief is to be retained or rejected in the future.[98]

Socialism had many affinities with Christianity, but the reality of God's active presence in the world had to inform it. Without recognizing God's greater Reality, socialism would be doomed to fail. Scudder put it this way: "Chaos; or slavery; these are the only alternatives to freedom signed with the holy sign. The Church is responsible as no other body for bearing this witness."[99]

In *Socialism and Character* she boldly stated: "The Church is never to be an end in itself."[100] The Church could educate Christians about the social situation and show the way to put that new knowledge into action. She envisioned this happening on both an individual level as well as through the collective life of the community. She called the Church to take seriously social Christianity and to create standards of Christian living for individuals to observe and for the life of the community to practice. Such standards should sound out the Spirit's distinctive voice rather than letting the speech of the world accent them.

Drawing upon God's model for the world evident in the Trinity and inspired by the voice of the Spirit, the Church could help shape a society built on the Christian principles of equality and democracy. To adopt the ethic of equality and democracy enlivened by the Spirit, the Church had a fourfold task: On an individual level, churches should (1) work on the inward spirituality of each member and (2) help all express that spiritual journey in outward action. As a community, the Church should (3) address the state of its membership and (4) define its outward mission in relation to the current social setting. The Church community itself should embody egalitarian values by welcoming all into its membership, including the working class.

Rauschenbusch sounded a similar call in *Christianity and the Social Crisis*. He invited the Church to align itself with the "rising class."[101] If Jesus witnessed the treatment of workers in the modern world, he would create a "new apostolate" that would share the burdens of poor as the first apostolate had done. The new apostolate would stand against oppressive structures that weighed down the poor and would sow the seeds of God's kingdom.

As a carrier of the Socialist Red Card, Scudder believed that a socialist society would allow Christians to express their convictions more fully. However, she did not equate Christian democracy with socialism or associate the Church merely with battles against what she called the worst "-isms." Writing to the Anglican Communion before its convention in 1919, she charged her Church to "keep abreast of truth."[102] The work of the Church was not to teach an unchanging ethic but "an ethic needing ever new application."[103] Christian democratic impulses had broken through false facades of worldly values found in every social movement from feudalism to capitalism. Scudder argued that "the new order of industrial democracy is upon us; and it is for the Church to supply this order with its distinctive soul."[104]

Practical expressions of Christian beliefs showed the inspiration of the Spirit of equality that had given life to the Church. To take a step in the right direction, she urged the Anglican Communion to show this democratic impulse in the makeup of its own community. Scudder was aware that Christians often expected the Church to solve the social problem, but they cannot think of the Church as an entity separate from its members. Individuals made up the community. Each person had a distinctive role to play. Like the cooperative Divine Society that inspired it, the individuals who composed the Church—bakers, millers, cobblers, mothers, and parsons—must decide how to work together inside and outside the confines of the Church's walls. A Church committed to an ethic of equality needed to focus more on equality in its own life. Scudder called upon the Church to make internal reforms and argued for a democratization of its body and practices. To structure itself in accord with the ethics of equality, the Church ought to invite the working class into its membership and show a real interest in the leadership of laypeople:

> Working men should be habitually sought out and appointed on vestries; women should be given a share in Church government; people should be permitted, through open forums or other means, to speak from the pews. It is a sad fact that few men are interested in being preached to; discussion rather than exhortation is the natural growth-organ of a democracy, and the Church should woo people to discuss.[105]

On different occasions Scudder enlisted the support of the Anglican Communion by inviting members to discuss at greater length the Church's stake in the social crisis. A well-seasoned social activist, Scudder lent her energies to a wide range of groups that made it their business to help the Church live up to its social mission. The Church League for Industrial Democracy (CLID), formed in 1919, was a good example of her work in this area. CLID became a particularly influential body and offered a safe forum in which Anglicans of diverse ideological persuasions discussed ways in which they could join forces to solve social problems.

Further, in *The Church and the Hour* Scudder argued that the Christian community spoke its distinctive language by expressing concern for the working class. Christians should shame those not buying Consumer's League Goods and any business owners unwilling to pay fair wages to their employees. Christians should shame them because these actions failed to express the nature of God, in whose image all human beings were made. Another way that the Church could work for social transformation was through prayer. A strong advocate of social intercession as a member of the Society of Companions of the Holy Cross, Scudder encouraged all Christians to petition sincerely for God's kingdom to come on earth, by praying for peace and fostering sound agricultural policies, social health, and economic justice.[106]

Women and the Cooperative Commonwealth

Although Scudder emphasized the importance of rectifying the inequalities of the economic system in order to solve the problems of classism, sexism, and racism, she also paid special attention to women's responsibility to bring about a more just social order. Part of a new generation of college-educated women and a professor at Wellesley College, she had an interest and investment in the relation of women to social need. She did not discuss women's responsibilities in terms of women's personal gain, yet one can deduce from her writings that women had the most to gain by the advent of a socialist state. Riding on a wave of social change, women had the opportunity to set an example for society.

Scudder sought to increase the sphere of women's influence by drawing upon women's distinctive experiences. She used women's leadership in the home as an example of the group consciousness and ability of women to nurture cooperation among family members. In the home, Scudder considered the needs of the whole above the needs of individuals. Her interest in defining a distinctive role for women to play in the social order extended to her vision for the Cooperative Commonwealth. That vision would transform a truly Cooperative Commonwealth into "the likeness of a home." Scudder effectively argued for the extension of women's roles to the public square, but she did little to revise the cultural connection society made between women, home, and family. She did not radically reconceive of women's roles; instead, she made women's private roles public. Women were the strongest and best-prepared leaders for the Cooperative Commonwealth because they had already been modeling cooperative behavior and leadership in the home.

College Women and Social Need

When Scudder joined Wellesley's faculty in 1887, the college was still working out its concept of higher education for women. Would it teach women so that they could adequately educate their sons to participate in the public domain? Or, would it prepare women themselves to influence and contribute to the social order? Patricia Palmieri points out that though women had attended seminaries since the 1820s, when Wellesley was founded the general public still perceived higher education for women as a social experiment.[107] The insignia Henry Durant, the college's founder, chose for Wellesley fit the public's perception: "Incipit Vita Nova" (The New Life Begins). But what would this "new life" for women entail?

Victorian society had severely restricted women's roles and limited much of their influence to the home. Society controlled the activities of "proper" women by teaching them to follow an intricate set of rules related to every aspect of their existence: eating habits, courtship, dress, home management, childbearing, and childrearing. Fashion that society recommended for women was symbolic of the restrictions placed upon them. Harvey Green recounted Frances Willard's feelings about the loss of freedom that she experienced when she reached adolescence:

> This is my birthday and the date of my martyrdom. Mother insists that at last I must have my hair "done up woman-fashion." My "back" hair is twisted up like a corkscrew; I carry eighteen hairpins; my head aches miserably; my feet are entangled in the skirt of my hateful new gown. I can never jump over a fence again, so long as I live.[108]

For much of the Victorian era, society succeeded in containing women, but by the late nineteenth century attitudes toward women were beginning to change. The growing interest in social change spurred reform movements that provided women with a much-needed boost to get across many of the fences separating them from the public arena.

The development of Wellesley's curriculum and educational philosophy coincided with the evolution of a variety of movements for social reform. Palmieri stated, "Wellesley College was very much a part of the larger romantic reform tradition and the quest for women's equality."[109] Early in its history Wellesley leaned toward a seminary model of education, under the leadership of President Ada Howard, a Mount Holyoke graduate. Durant chose her for the position because she would enforce the somewhat extensive list of regulations that he outlined for the students. The seminary model for education impressed Durant, a onetime member of the board of directors of Mount Holyoke Seminary. However, he was also attracted to cutting-edge movements for social reform and experimented with education in ways that flouted tradition. Wellesley created a good atmosphere for observing social experimentation. It tested the latest reform trends, including fads related to diet, health, women's dress, and academic study. Taking a cue from German universities, Wellesley built laboratories that were even the envy of male colleges. The most radical experiment of all was the appointment of an all-women faculty. In the late nineteenth century an all-female faculty and president made Wellesley stand out as a distinctive voice among women's colleges.[110] In the end, Howard proved to be poorly suited to steer the progressive institution. Students and faculty attracted to the college because of its reputation for social experimentation did not feel encouraged by a president characterized as "the emblem of the submissive woman."[111] The next president, Alice Freeman, a graduate of the University of Michigan, was a better fit for the position. Freeman embodied the reform-minded woman by infusing "the genteel womanly style of behavior with a forceful, almost despotic will."[112] She secured Wellesley's future as a college that would progress far beyond the women's seminary model.

Appointed to the faculty under Freeman's leadership, Scudder had the opportunity to influence Wellesley's conception of education for women in a significant way:

> For Vida Scudder a college course would allow a woman to develop some unity in her life—to move through middle age with purpose. It would bring a balance to female adolescence; it would be an antidote to the dissipation of energy characteristic of middle-class women and to the emptiness caused by the lack of a valid and authentic social role. Higher education that culminated in productivity—a career—would bring a woman's life stability instead of futility.[113]

According to Scudder, there was "no better training-school in practical democracy than a woman's College."[114]

Teresa Corcoran called attention to a sense of ambivalence toward the character and role of women in Scudder's earlier articles.[115] In her series of essays on "The Educated Woman as a Social Factor," Scudder viewed higher education as a means toward giving young women a better approach to their home duties as well as a way for them to contribute to the social order. College women did not have to eliminate marriage as an alternative. It was just not their only alternative.[116] As Scudder continued to question traditional women's roles, she gradually defined a clearer concept of womanhood. College education would produce a "new womanhood," through which women would impact the public domain.

In her keen analysis of womanhood in modern poetry, Scudder observed how attitudes toward women were changing. Comparing modern poetry to that of Shakespeare, she argued that modern poets presented women with greater depth and complexity:

> Widely, indeed, does the conception of the modern differ from that of the Elizabethan artist. To Shakespeare, women are things ensky'd and sainted; to Browning, they are suffering human souls. The modern poet sees them, not as separated from men in the calm of attainment, but as sharing with them in the perpetual struggle which is the condition of humanity.
>
> . . . Women are no longer, as in the days of chivalry, placed upon remote heights, there to be adored from afar; they are brought face to face with the very turmoil of existence, in the world and in their own hearts.[117]

Robert Browning best exemplified the new attitude toward women in modern poetry. His work showed three traits characteristic of modern poetry: it gave less emphasis to love between a man and a woman; it placed greater emphasis on moral and spiritual loveliness than physical attraction; and it depicted women as themselves rather than through the eyes of their lovers.[118] Unlike Shakespeare, female characters in Browning's poems wrestled with deeper issues and conflict. Scudder also suggested, however, that though modern poets like Browning presented somewhat more realistic depictions of women, woman's nature in Shakespeare and Browning remained essentially the same. For both poets, "woman knows a moral pre-eminence, and her office in life is at once to inspire and to serve."[119] It was this theme of the ethical elements of womanhood that Scudder developed when considering college women's leadership in the modern world.

College-educated women represented a new factor in the social order. Born into a world on the cusp of social change, Scudder defined their purpose in relation to obvious social needs. Broadening earlier boundaries, she speculated about what society would gain if college women exerted their "feminine instincts" upon it:

> Think what might be the result if the force of self-sacrifice, inherent in half of humanity, should spend itself no longer in often misdirected ardor within the narrow limits of individual lives, but should work in intelligent subordination to perceived justice, and turn toward the solution of broad social problems. The result, on the whole, cannot be predicted; it would not, perhaps, be the collectivist millennium, but it might be a perceptible trend toward greater equality and fairness in the social order.[120]

Higher education, she thought, aimed to arouse women's sensibilities toward social issues and trained them to address social needs in practical ways.[121]

Scudder emphasized women's spirituality when contemplating the relation of college women to social need and sought to expand the boundaries of the "guiding and purifying power of essential womanhood."[122] Women were well equipped to address social problems because they had already learned to nurture an inward devotion to God:

> Thus do the women of the new order promise, as I believe, to possess the exact union of elements which the times demand for the interpretation of their need, and for its cure: the willingness for personal service, joined with wisdom and control; the emphasis on moral and sympathetic elements as factors

> in human life, mingled with perception of practical possibilities and of the sacredness of law.[123]

Corcoran suggested that Scudder's novels clearly showed her view of women's role and character. In *The Disciple of a Saint*, Scudder reflected on her own spiritual journey through a story recording the adventures of Neri, Catherine of Siena's scribe. In the preface to the book, Scudder admitted that the story is an effort to draw the reader closer to Catherine. Catherine taught Neri about the interconnection between spirituality and the pursuit of social change. Catherine, a leader of the Church in a time of schism, worked toward Christian unity and advanced social change. In *On Journey* Scudder wrote:

> Catherine seemed to me the prototype of all modern women idealists. . . . We see her gradually called to larger activities in the most important phases of civic and international life; she reminded me of Jane Addams, but with a difference. For if Catherine was a great statesman, she was also a great Contemplative. And all the time, very woman.[124]

Not all Social Gospelers shared Scudder's high view of what society might gain from feminine spirituality. Ely thought that churches could begin to address the social situation only by dealing with the problems caused by a Church composed predominately of women. In the late nineteenth century male church attendance had significantly declined. Ely linked the decline in the social aspect of the Church's mission to an emphasis on feminine spirituality:

> The trouble is that she [the church] has in recent centuries to a large extent been preaching a one-sided half-gospel, and not a whole gospel. The remedy is a strong masculine gospel, and not merely a feminine gospel; in other words, a whole gospel.[125]

For Scudder, however, the fact that women were already well prepared inwardly was a tremendous asset to count on when addressing social needs. Her involvement in the settlement movement showed her attitude toward women's preparation and potential to address social problems. Social settlements provided important avenues for women to follow Jesus' mandate and to live out their Christian commitment to address social concerns. Women who worked in the settlement movements built a bridge between the widening gap of the rich and the poor: "Only through a fellowship of the free and strong—founded on sympathy, it may be on sacrifice—can the life of the rich be enlarged, can the life of the poor be uplifted, sweetened, and brightened."[126]

In many ways Scudder's notion of the "new womanhood" paralleled Rauschenbusch's concept of the "new apostolate." Like the "new apostolate," new women had a special consciousness of God's great social commission to the whole of humanity. Women were to sow the seeds of social change by working in the public sphere. Scudder more closely linked "feminine" spiritual instincts to the pursuit of radical social change than did Rauschenbusch, but both were clear that a "new apostolate" and a "new womanhood" were to "rally sufficient religious faith and moral strength to snap the bonds of evil and turn the present unparalleled economic and intellectual resources of humanity to the harmonious development of a true social life."[127]

Settlement work provided a connection between Scudder's academic, social, and spiritual interests. Settlements imported from other places things that impoverished communities lacked. They did not function as Christian missions per se but enabled workers to embody their personal sense of mission:

> The settlement is vitalized by a religious motive and faith; but while its members are free to express themselves religiously and politically in accordance with their convictions, the settlement as a group is through its associated life gathering convictions rather than expressing them.[128]

The ultimate goal for the settlement was to build up a common life between residents and their neighbors. Programming, however, was not usually religious. Among other things, Scudder and Dudley organized a social science club at Denison House in 1893 and sponsored lectures on topics such as "The Ethics of Trade Unions" and "German Socialism."

Settlement work expanded the horizons of the impoverished and broadened the perspectives of the residents, as Scudder claimed:

> That training has a distinct value. Its best result is to take us out of the circle of purely personal and immediate interests, to teach our relations with past and future, with the great outer world, to enlarge consciousness till we recognize ourselves as parts—responsible parts—of that national life which one of our wisest men has manifested to us as a Moral Organism. If one member suffers, all other members suffer with it.[129]

In *Twenty Years at Hull House* fellow settlement worker Addams admitted that "the first generation of college women had taken their learning too quickly, . . . that the contemporary education of young women had developed too exclusively the power of acquiring knowledge and of merely receiving impressions."[130] She agreed with Scudder that educated women had to encounter poverty if it was to change them. Those living in settlement houses experienced firsthand the hopelessness of the poor and began to understand the real need for a cooperative fellowship in society.

Eventually Scudder separated herself from the social settlement movement. Believing that her reputation as a social radical might impede the work of Denison House, she left the future of its work in the trustworthy hands of her colleague Helena Dudley. Marilyn Howley Smith characterizes her ultimate disillusionment with the settlements as shattered hope:

> Scudder could no longer escape the realization that the movement had not brought the particular kind of sweeping social change she had envisioned. Moreover, she was moving toward an ever more radical social vision and the settlement movement was becoming more of a sociological experiment which did not suit her temperament or goals.[131]

Scudder realized that the settlements as they were conceived could not accomplish enough. They raised awareness about the problems of the poor in urban areas but fell short when trying to establish a basis for radical social change.

Over the duration of Scudder's forty-year tenure at Wellesley, she tended a blossoming garden of young women who would contribute to the world much "beyond our old limits of the domestic circle and social clique."[132] As a professor she fed her students intellectually so that they might grow freely into their own ideas. About her students she wrote, "Teachers should create in them the illusion of freedom, as the Almighty creates in the human race."[133] Her method was to open within students a pathway for their own "imprisoned splendor"[134] to escape. Reflecting on the significance of higher education for women, Scudder said, "The most important immediate change it has brought is doubtless the introduction of purpose into feminine life."[135]

Scudder befriended many of her students but developed a long-lasting friendship with Florence Converse, to whom she dedicated two of her most significant books, *Socialism and Character* and *On Journey*.[136] Also a visionary, Converse expressed her social concerns in creative ways. She published a book of collected poems that bore the imprint of her socialist commitments.[137] Palmieri discussed Scudder's and Converse's friendship in relation to Wellesley as a group of women committed to women. She recognized that some people speculated about relationships between women faculty and their female friends. Single faculty members often entered what Palmieri termed "Wellesley marriages," where relationships with other women replaced traditional family models.

Women and the New Social Order

In an article for *Yale Review* entitled "Woman and Socialism," Scudder contemplated the specific relationship of women to her vision for the Cooperative Commonwealth. Here, Scudder's distinctive voice emerged from the ranks of both Social Gospelers and Socialists. Socialists had pushed the property question to the forefront of the discussion. Quoting Victor Berger, Scudder underscored the dominant socialist position:

> "The sex question," says he, in words remembered rather than accurately quoted, "is for the twenty-first century, not for us. Ours is the property question, and it is foolish and feeble to try to solve both at the same time."[138]

Though she disliked segregated conversations of women as women,[139] she admitted that society needed to attend to the relation of sex to public affairs. She agreed with Berger's emphasis on the question of property, but what Berger had failed to recognize in his statement was that society often treated women as property. With the social change that was in process, gender was an important issue in the public square.

Indeed, from Scudder's point of view, a thorough investigation of society's treatment of women strengthened the socialist indictment of capitalism. She considered the socially accepted views of marital relationships and pointed out that people generally thought of married women as the property of their husbands. They had interpreted marriage as a kind of legalized slavery. Hurled into the cold and unfriendly job market created by industrial society, women were given no more room to succeed. Industry wasted their talents, health, strength, and capacity. At the other end of the spectrum, wealthy women, prized for their appearance and charm, were demoralized by their superficial duties. Looking at these conditions left no doubt that women stood to gain a great deal from the emergence of a new state.

Scudder pointed out that socialist organizations were some of the first to give women equal voice and vote. The party practiced suffrage for women internationally. As a result the number of women who identified themselves among the ranks of the socialists increased. Between 1909 and 1911 in

Germany, women's membership in the Socialist Party grew from 29,459 to 82,045.[140] Letters that American women wrote to Rauschenbusch attested to their surging interest in the Socialist Party. Caroline Pelleburton declared: "For some years past, I have been calling myself a Socialist and have been known as such. I joined the Phila Socialist Party—a working-class organization."[141] One woman even attributed her commitment to socialism to his arguments outlined in *Christianity and the Social Crisis*: "Ever since I read the book a year ago, Christianity has been so much more of a love and a motive to me and socialism has become the Christian's opportunity."[142]

Scudder believed that the pursuit of equality for women was inherent within the socialist vision for society. Socialists believed in the transference of society from a competitive order to a cooperative order, and they conceived of the state as the mother of society, not a police officer:

> The result is that we are all feeling our way towards the conception of a government whose function shall be no longer to restrict but to evoke energy: less to suppress impulses that threaten the common good, than to allure its children towards production, towards creation.[143]

The socialist state would be life-giving and lure all of its children to produce, even its women.

Women already operated on a cooperative basis. Scudder emphasized the fact that women "bring the whole race into the world to begin with, which is no small enterprise; they play the chief part in fostering and educating it; and they make its homes."[144] Socialists aimed to deemphasize financial gain as the motivation for contributing to society. The affections of their family rather than profit for their labor rewarded women. Scudder further argued that women had a "group-consciousness far more evolved than that of men."[145] As the traditional nurturers of family life, they had shaped and controlled a smaller version of a cooperative society. The home met the basic needs of all members of the family, with the good of the whole family in mind; family members possessed goods in communal fashion. In sum, much of the socialist vision for society echoed the best of women's experiences.

Scudder resonated with Rauschenbusch's sentiments about the family as one of the most valuable institutions in modern life. "The family," Rauschenbusch wrote, "is the structural cell of the social organism."[146] Like the Church and the state, the family was "communistic."[147] It may seem odd that Scudder and Rauschenbusch identified the family as a communistic institution when they were both well aware that families did not operate on a total basis of equality. Women played a large role, greater than that of men, in nurturing the home environment, but they did not receive equal legal status. Scudder and Rauschenbusch agreed, however, that the end of the family was to live in harmony with one another and to hold goods and property in common, even though the means to achieve this end needed improvement. Most important, the family exemplified a group of people who used limited resources and yielded the best moral character possible for each of its members.

While both Rauschenbusch and Scudder emphasized the importance of women's leadership roles in the family, they parted ways when considering the role that these leaders would play in transforming the social order. Scudder saw the expansion of women's influence beyond the home as the force that would create a more cooperative society. Rauschenbusch lamented the entry of women into the industrial workforce because that might undercut the contribution they made to the home as spiritual leaders. He questioned whether or not the opening of so many women to new professions was progress. In his mind, women experienced more independence, but it came at too great a price to them and to society:

> Some educated girls think they prefer the practice of a profession because the dream of unusual success lures them; but when they have had a taste of wearing routine that prevails in most professions, they turn with longing to the thought of a home of their own. Our industrial machine has absorbed the functions which women formerly fulfilled in the home, and has drawn them into its hopper because female labor is unorganized and cheap labor. They are made to compete with the very men who ought to marry them, and thus they further diminish their own chance of marriage. If any one has a sound reason for taking the competitive system by the throat in righteous wrath, it is the unmarried woman and the mother with girls.[148]

Rauschenbusch reluctantly advocated for the woman's movement because he thought that if women were going to be part of the workforce, they had the right to argue for fair wages and equal treatment. Unlike Scudder, he felt anxious about how women would handle their newfound freedom.[149]

Scudder did not share Rauschenbusch's reluctance about women's entry into the workforce or dialogue about public policy. She enthusiastically endorsed the emergence of women into the public domain. Drawing upon their feminine instincts, women were well prepared to take their place beside men to bring into being the mother state:

They have the vision of Justice, and they rejoice to aid in the task that lies before us—the task, which socialism understands more definitely than any other phase of the reform movement, of transforming society from the likeness of a battlefield to the likeness of a home.[150]

Notes

1. Parts of this chapter were previously published as an article, "A New Womanhood: Vida Dutton Scudder on Women's Public Role in Advancing the Social Gospel," in *Perspectives in Religious Studies.*
2. Vida Dutton Scudder, "The Social Conscience of the Future: I," *The Hibbert Journal* 7 (January 1909): 317.
3. Vida Dutton Scudder, "Socialism and Spiritual Progress—A Speculation," An address delivered before the Society of Christian Socialists, Boston, March 1891, 1.
4. Vida Dutton Scudder, *Socialism and Character* (Boston: Houghton, Mifflin, 1912), 192.
5. Vida Dutton Scudder, *On Journey* (New York: Dutton, 1937), 162.
6. Vida Dutton Scudder, *A Listener in Babel* (Boston: Houghton, Mifflin, 1903), 115.
7. Richard T. Ely, *Socialism and Social Reform* (New York: T. Y. Crowell, 1894), 24.
8. George Bernard Shaw, ed., *The Fabian Essays in Socialism* (1889; repr., London: George Allen & Unwin, 1950), 32.
9. Vida Dutton Scudder, "Socialism and Sacrifice," *The Atlantic Monthly* 105 (June 1910): 838.
10. Scudder, *Socialism and Character*, 120.
11. Ibid., 132.
12. Ibid., 123.
13. Scudder, "Socialism and Sacrifice," 14.
14. Ibid., 22.
15. See Georg Lukács, *History and Class Consciousness: Studies in Marxist Dialectics* (trans. Rodney Livingstone; Cambridge, MA: MIT Press, 1971), 46–82.
16. See Scudder, "Class Consciousness," *The Atlantic Monthly* 107 (March 1911): 323.
17. Scudder, *Socialism and Character*, 162.
18. Scudder, "Class Consciousness," 329.
19. Scudder, *Socialism and Character*, 154.
20. Ibid., 178.
21. Ibid.
22. Scudder, "Class Consciousness," 323.
23. Scudder, *Socialism and Character*, 65.
24. See Ira Kipnis, *The American Socialist Movement, 1897–1912* (New York: Columbia University Press, 1952).
25. Scudder, "The Social Conscience of the Future: I," 314.
26. Scudder, *On Journey*, 302.
27. Jane Addams, *Twenty Years at Hull House* (New York: Macmillan, 1911), 186.
28. Ibid., 187.
29. Scudder, "Class Consciousness," 320.
30. Vida Dutton Scudder to Walter Rauschenbusch, September 21, 1912. Walter Rauschenbusch Papers, Box 93, American Baptist Historical Society Manuscript Collection, Samuel Colgate Historical Library, Colgate Rochester Divinity School, Rochester, NY.

31. Anthony Pinn, ed., *Making the Gospel Plain: The Writings of Bishop Reverdy C. Ransom* (Harrisburg: Trinity Press International, 1999), 187.

32. See Arthur Mann, *Yankee Reformers in an Urban Age* (Cambridge, MA: Harvard University Press, 1954).

33. Vida Dutton Scudder, "Democracy and Education," *The Atlantic Monthly* 89 (June 1902): 820.

34. Vida Dutton Scudder, "A Glimpse into Life," *The Wellesley Magazine* 1 (February 18, 1893): 224.

35. See Oscar Handlin, *Boston's Immigrants, 1790–1880: A Study in Acculturation* (New York: Atheneum, 1972), 54–150.

36. Scudder, "A Glimpse into Life," 227.

37. Scudder, *A Listener in Babel*, 109.

38. Fragment of newspaper clipping found in Scudder Files, Archives of the Society of Companion of the Holy Cross, Adelynrood, South Byfield, MA.

39. Scudder, *A Listener in Babel*, 109.

40. Scudder, *On Journey*, 185.

41. See "Miss Scudder's Criticized Speech: Just What She Said at a Citizens' Meeting in Lawrence, to Which Exception Has Been so Excitedly Taken by the Brahmins," *The Boston Common*, March 9, 1912, 6–7 (clipping found in Scudder Papers, Wellesley College Archives, Margaret Clapp Library, Wellesley College, Wellesley, MA).

42. See Walter Rauschenbusch, *Christianizing the Social Order* (New York: Macmillan, 1912), 249.

43. Scudder, *Socialism and Character*, 191.

44. Scudder, *A Listener in Babel*, 117.

45. Vida Dutton Scudder, "The College Settlements Movement," *Smith College Monthly* 7 (May 1900): 448.

46. Paul T. Phillips, *A Kingdom on Earth: Anglo-American Social Christianity, 1880–1940* (University Park, PA: The Pennsylvania State University Press, 1996), 100.

47. Scudder, *Socialism and Character*, 207.

48. Ibid., 211.

49. Ibid., 212.

50. Scudder, *On Journey*, 181–82.

51. Letter from Caroline Hazard to Vida Dutton Scudder, June 7, 1900. Scudder Papers, Wellesley College Archives, Margaret Clapp Library, Wellesley College, Wellesley, MA.

52. Scudder, *Socialism and Character*, 211.

53. Ibid., 216.

54. Ibid., 218.

55. Ibid., 220.

56. Ibid., 239.

57. Ibid., 200.

58. Scudder, "The Social Conscience of the Future: I," 328.

59. Ibid.

60. Karl Marx, *Capital, The Communist Manifesto and Other Writings* (New York: The Modern Library, 1959), 318.

61. Scudder, "The Social Conscience of the Future: I," 315, with emphasis added.

62. Scudder, *Socialism and Character*, 130.

63. David Ricardo, *The Principles of Political Economy and Taxation* (1911; repr., London: Everyman's Library, 1965), 61.

64. Scudder, *Socialism and Character*, 138.

65. Ibid., 193.
66. Ibid., 205.
67. Ibid.
68. Ibid., 188.
69. Ibid., 129.
70. Ibid., 185.
71. See Vida Dutton Scudder, "The Doubting Pacifist," *The Yale Review* 6 (July 1917): 738–51.
72. Vida Dutton Scudder, "Franciscan Parallels," *Anglican Theological Review* 5 (March 1923): 296.
73. Vida Dutton Scudder, ". . . The Price of Liberty," *The Commonweal* 27 (April 15, 1938): 681.
74. Ibid.
75. Ibid.
76. Ibid., 682.
77. Scudder, *Socialism and Character*, 243.
78. Ibid.
79. Ibid., 242.
80. Ibid.
81. Ibid., 258.
82. Ibid., 251.
83. Ibid., 252.
84. Ibid., 249.
85. Ibid., 255.
86. Ibid.
87. Ibid., 268.
88. Ibid., 271.
89. Scudder, "The Social Conscience of the Future: I," 321.
90. Ibid., 326.
91. Vida Dutton Scudder, "The Church and Social Rebirth: The Final of a Series," *The Witness* 30 (December 4, 1947): 9.
92. Ibid., 11.
93. Vida Dutton Scudder, *The Church and the Hour* (New York: Dutton, 1917), 4.
94. Vida Dutton Scudder, "The Alleged Failure of the Church to Meet the Social Emergency," in *The Church and the Hour*, 60.
95. See Walter Rauschenbusch, *Christianity and the Social Crisis* (1907; repr., Louisville: Westminster/John Knox Press, 1991), 143–210.
96. See Vida Dutton Scudder, "Democracy and the Church," *The Atlantic Monthly* 90 (October 1902): 521–27; and idem, *The Church and the Hour*, 114.
97. Vida Dutton Scudder, "How Draw Workingmen to Church?" *The American Church Monthly* 4 (September 1918): 28.
98. Vida Dutton Scudder, "The Waiting Task," *Christendom* (London) 1 (June 1931): 123.
99. Scudder, "The Church and Social Rebirth," 11.
100. Scudder, *Socialism and Character*, 380.
101. Rauschenbusch, *Christianity and the Social Crisis*, 414.
102. Vida Dutton Scudder, "The Church Today," *Anglican Theological Review* 2 (October 1919): 106.
103. Ibid., 108.
104. Ibid.

105. Ibid., 112.
106. Vida Dutton Scudder, *The Church and Social Justice* (New York: The National Council, Department of Christian Social Service, 1934): 7.
107. Patricia Palmieri, *In Adamless Eden* (New Haven: Yale University Press, 1995), 4.
108. Harvey Green, *The Light of the Home: An Intimate View of the Lives of Women in Victorian America* (New York: Pantheon Books, 1983), 10.
109. Palmieri, *In Adamless Eden*, 10.
110. Ibid., 1–34.
111. Ibid., 13.
112. Ibid., 20.
113. Ibid., 152.
114. Vida Dutton Scudder, "Notes from Denison House," *Smith College Monthly* 3, no. 6 (March 1896): 42.
115. Teresa Corcoran, *Vida Dutton Scudder* (Boston: Twayne, 1982), 102.
116. Vida Dutton Scudder, "The Educated Woman as a Social Factor: III," *The Christian Union* 35 (April 14, 1887): 12.
117. Vida Dutton Scudder, "Womanhood in Modern Poetry," *Poet Lore* 1 (October 15, 1889): 461.
118. Ibid., 452.
119. Ibid., 465.
120. Scudder, "The Educated Woman as a Social Factor: III," 13.
121. Ibid.
122. Scudder, "Womanhood in Modern Poetry," 465.
123. Vida Dutton Scudder, *The Relation of College Women to Social Need* (Association of Collegiate Alumnae Publications, series 2, no. 3; n.p., 1890), 5.
124. Scudder, *On Journey*, 243.
125. Richard Ely, *The Social Aspects of Christianity* (New York: Thomas Y. Crowell, 1889), 148.
126. Scudder, *The Relation of College Women to Social Need*, 9.
127. Rauschenbusch, *Christianity and the Social Crisis*, 422.
128. Mary Simkhovitch, "The Settlement and Religion," in *Readings in the Development of Settlement Work* (ed. Lorene M. Pacey; New York: Association, 1950), 142.
129. Scudder, *The Relation of College Women to Social Need*, 6.
130. Jane Addams, *Twenty Years at Hull House* (New York: Macmillan, 1911), 71.
131. Marilyn Howley Smith, "Vida Dutton Scudder and Social Reform: A Theology of Hope" (PhD diss., St. Louis University, 1996), 115.
132. Vida Dutton Scudder, "A Pedagogic Sunset," *The Atlantic Monthly* 141 (June 1928): 782.
133. Ibid., 785.
134. Ibid., 786.
135. Ibid., 782.
136. Palmieri, *In Adamless Eden*, 137–42.
137. See Florence Converse, *Collected Poems of Florence Converse* (New York: Dutton, 1937).
138. Vida Dutton Scudder, "Woman and Socialism," *The Yale Review* 3 (April 1914): 456.
139. Scudder, *On Journey*, 64.
140. Scudder, "Woman and Socialism," 459.

141. Caroline Pelleburton to Walter Rauschenbusch, January 27, 1908. Walter Rauschenbusch Papers, American Baptist Historical Society Manuscript Collection, Samuel Colgate Historical Library, Colgate Rochester Divinity School, Rochester, NY.
142. Anna Rochester to Walter Rauschenbusch, March 23, 1909. Walter Rauschenbusch Papers, American Baptist Historical Society Manuscript Collection, Samuel Colgate Historical Library, Colgate Rochester Divinity School, Rochester, NY.
143. Scudder, "Woman and Socialism," 460.
144. Ibid., 461.
145. Ibid., 463.
146. Rauschenbusch, *Christianity and the Social Crisis*, 271.
147. Ibid., 414.
148. Ibid., 276–77.
149. See Walter Rauschenbusch, "Is the Woman's Movement Going to Save Society?" *Ford Hall Folks* 2, no. 28 (April 26, 1914): 1–4.
150. Scudder, "Woman and Socialism," 470.

4
Scudder's Moral Reasoning, Sources, and Norms

Four key elements provided the framework for Scudder's orientation toward social reform and supported her arguments for specific policy changes that would ensure the restructuring of the social order. These elements included (1) her interpretation of the social circumstances that called for moral involvement; (2) her view of human nature and the ability of human beings to affect social change; (3) her moral values, norms, and guidelines; and (4) the loyalties or causes to be served by the policies for which she advocated. Taking a closer look at the interaction of these four elements further illumines the theological basis for Scudder's reformism and demonstrates how she thought a mutually beneficial partnership between Christianity and socialism would improve the social order. Scudder reconsidered the current orientation of social policy in an effort to transform the social order in light of God's cooperative image. Common ownership of property and the means of production, stricter labor regulations, suffrage for women, and ultimately the elimination of all forms of social competition, especially war—all these were policies that would achieve the goal of establishing a more cooperative society; the Cooperative Commonwealth.

An Environment That Nurtured "Instincts of Defiant Self-Protection"

Scudder measured the condition of a society crippled by the spread of capitalism and class antagonism against the ideal of a socialist alternative. In sum, economics determined the value of individuals to the social whole. Competitive capitalism rewarded individualism and nurtured what she called "instincts of defiant self-protection," thereby encouraging greater social stratification. Clearly, one of her main points was that the rampant individualism furthered by competition corrupted the social institutions themselves. Capitalism favored benefits for the wealthy at the expense of the poor. To a great extent, industrialists treated the working class unfairly. These wretched conditions negatively impacted individual character and encouraged people to act out of concern for their own interests rather than out of consideration for the common good. Competition nurtured the growth of a double ethic. Social classes developed into different moral types according to the varying conditions of race and class. Scudder believed that the moral health of the nation was in grave danger.

Developing economic and social theories enabled Scudder to see this moral problem in light of the malleability of social institutions. She believed that institutions and individuals could progress beyond the corruption of prevalent social practices and evolve toward the greater economic and religious freedom experienced in a truly egalitarian society. Once leaders had diagnosed moral ailments, they could remedy them. Under the right conditions society could progress toward a true ethic of equality and return the nation to moral health. The enactment of socialist policies would alleviate the moral strain imposed upon all classes by competition.

Scudder always worked out her understanding of current circumstances against the background of a vision of a Cooperative Commonwealth informed by her theology. Kept in the back of her mind was the idea that God represented true democracy. The Trinity was the ultimate witness to true democracy. Humanity was made in the image of God's creative and cooperative life known in the Three-in-One.

Directly related to this point was the idea that individual well-being was not only tied up with the well-being of the human community but also intricately related to the search to know God. God could not feel at home with a people forcibly tied to material goods and consumed by their interest in financial achievement, at the expense of their quest for spiritual discernment. The incarnation made it clear that it was natural for God to love and to seek relationship with humanity. Moreover, it was natural for human beings to love and live in real relationship with one another.

Society would better reflect God's cooperative image as it embodied the equality and love known in God. Christ taught the principles by which society could more closely approximate this vision by pronouncing its blessing on the poor, the meek, and the hungry. The Cooperative Commonwealth would not free society from suffering—physical, mental, or spiritual—but all would highly regard solidarity with the poor laborer and an interest in equality, justice, and community. Socialism would create an environment in which it could base society on authentic democratic principles. This was the cause for which she worked.

According to Scudder, Christians had been given a special charge to live as an inspiration to the new social order. The Church was society's best hope for achieving God's vision of society. The Spirit inspired Christians to work for democracy and social equality. Scudder identified that pursuit with the ideals of the Socialist Party: "Does it mean nothing that our Whitsun altars glow with red? Might not the Red flag find itself at home there?"[1]

Consistently Scudder referred to the Spirit's inspiration of the Christian Socialist in her work. In *Socialism and Character*, where she thought of socialism as a movement inspired by the Spirit, Scudder thought that the Catholic Church would be most successful in the socialist state because it already encouraged Christians to nurture their inner selves. The Christian religion would nurture the inner self, making better socialists, and socialism would provide a better environment for Christianity:

> These social institutions would afford the natural soil in which they and the kindred doctrine of a Holy Spirit, indwelling in nature, and more especially in consecrated humanity, could flourish; the doctrines in their turn would give exactly the needed sanction to democratic and yet more socialistic theory.[2]

Both socialism and Christianity would influence one another, bringing about changes in their present conceptions.

Over the duration of Scudder's life, society and social needs changed a great deal. After joining the Socialist Party in 1911, her commitment to socialism never wavered, but her conception of socialism expanded, particularly in the years following World War One. More in-depth study of St. Francis and his followers further clarified the origin of the Church's stake in working for social revolution. By the 1930s, she denied the title of political communist. After witnessing the events of newly revolutionized Russia, she distanced herself entirely from brands of socialism associated with materialism. She made her case plain in an article on "Christian Citizenship" published in 1934. The greatest difference between Marxist and Christian social visions was in the means toward social change. Christians and Marxists held in common the pursuit of an egalitarian society, but the materialism, violence, cruelty, and suppression of freedom associated with Continental Communism shocked and outraged Scudder.[3] Real social revolution would be born of the Spirit, not out of concern for worldly goods.

Communism had marched its way onto the global scene, but Scudder's vision of the Cooperative Commonwealth was never realized; the world had not met a socialist state informed by Christian principles. Nearing the end of her life, she still wondered about the moral gain that could be achieved if a real partnership had been created:

> But what if Communism were Christianized? Isn't it through the union of opposites that all progress is made? Communism and Sacramental Christianity need each other more and more, as some people are discovering. Their union releases Communism from the dangerous totalitarian method that uses compulsion, and [releases] Christianity from the insidious disguised indolence and egotism that lazily avoid the call to corporate action.[4]

Created in God's Cooperative Image

Scudder's view of human nature deeply informed her interpretation of the social circumstances calling for moral involvement and her arguments for public policy. Like Fabian Sidney Webb, Scudder was well aware that social conditions shaped human beings, and that pressure beyond the individuals themselves played a significant role in the shaping of their moral character. Webb discussed this in terms of the relationship between the individual and the social organism. He argued that the social organism evolved from the union of individuals, and that in turn the social system created individuals. Life in society was born of a larger life, and social pressure molded the attributes of that society and its individual members.[5] For Scudder, her theological anthropology informed the idea of life in society being born of a larger life. Her anthropological assumptions attested to her deep and abiding search to understand the relationship between God, individuals, and the social organism as a whole.

Basing her understanding of human nature on her concept of God, Scudder affirmed that human beings were inherently social beings. Human beings depended upon God for their creation, yet at the same time they were responsible for the social order. As moral agents, they did not create moral forces; they reshaped them. She shared the optimism of many Social Gospelers about the ability of humanity to achieve their social ends, but like Rauschenbusch, she also recognized human limitations.

Christian doctrine taught Scudder that human beings were made in the image of God. Current sociological and economic theories illumined Scudder's interpretation of that doctrine. She surmised that the meaning of the doctrine of the Trinity for the modern age rested in its revelation of God as a social being. Creator, Christ, and Holy Spirit worked cooperatively to promote a Divine Society based on equality and love. The doctrine of being created in this cooperative image affirmed that human beings themselves were social and existed not to promote their own individual well-being but to live in fellowship. Human beings were incomplete without one another and shared God's longing to live in a cooperative society. The doctrine of the Trinity also affirmed God's desire to live in fellowship with humanity and thereby revealed humanity's need to live in fellowship with the God who created them.

These basic affirmations about human nature provided the foundation for Scudder's attitude toward public policy and the basis upon which she could build her interpretation of the circumstances calling for moral involvement. If human beings were inherently social, then social systems and policies that valued individuality over the common good ran counter to human nature. Not only did such individualistic institutions misunderstand human beings, they also served as an impediment for a life lived in fellowship with God. Therefore, society needed to radically alter itself so that human beings could live into their full potential.

Social Responsibility and Essential Human Nature

For Scudder, being made in the image of God also implied a sense of responsibility for the social order. Scudder turned to the incarnation to explain more fully the essential nature of humanity. God's manifestation in human flesh not only showed the extent to which God longed to live in community but also showed God's voluntary limitations. God extended Godself beyond natural boundaries to be in relationship with those who were truly other. In doing so, God voluntarily subjected Godself to human cooperation to accomplish God's intentions. Human beings were dependent upon God for their creation, but God also needed them. Here, Scudder looked to the role a woman played in bringing Christ into the world as she explained that social responsibility was an essential aspect of human nature.

Looking at the incarnation from two angles, she remembered the significance of the celebration of Christmastide in *Social Teachings of the Christian Year*. Through the birth of Jesus Christ, God had redeemed humanity. A human mother had given birth to Jesus, and a community had prepared a place for Christ to be born in the world. Mary had carried, labored for, and given birth to Jesus. God had depended upon Mary, an earthen vessel, to fulfill God's purposes. God had "chosen to be weak, to be a babe in our arms, Whom if we will we may dash against the stones."[6] The incarnation reminded human beings of their own responsibility to mother God, "like the Virgin Mother, to bring forever to the birth the Savior of the world!"[7] These actions showed God's dependence upon people to bear redemption in the social order and humanity's potential to prepare a place for God:

> Humanity His Mother, asking that we who have brought Him to the birth, should nourish and cherish Him. Dependent on us—oh, mystic thought!—for the power to fulfill His purpose and make us whole, He seeks our nurturing love that it may bring him to the fullness of His Manhood.[8]

Recalling the story of Mary's trip to Bethlehem, Scudder observed that some people had prepared a place for the baby to be born; others had turned Mary away. The story's significance was not limited to the actual birth event but also understood in light of the crucifixion. In her words, "We must at Bethlehem remember Calvary."[9] Scudder emphasized human activity as free agents, to choose whether or not to make a place for God to be at home in the world. "All those labors, which seek for the race a healthful and decent physical existence, are preparations that men may be born from above; it is our high privilege to make the social organism a fit home for the Indwelling God."[10]

This understanding of the essential activity of human beings to participate in God's redemption and to prepare a place for God in the world translated directly into her arguments for social reform:

> Behold, the Tabernacle of God is with men. Housing reform, sanitation, dietetics and the like, are all sanctified by the Incarnation. . . . Indifference to earthly life and satisfaction in it are alike denied to him who kneels before the Babe. To him, the world of sense is neither illusion nor enemy; but still less is it his object. It is the sacramental instrument of the Spirit, and he would fain ensure its health and purity with as anxious care as men show in preparation for the Eucharistic Host. All those labors, which seek for the race a healthful and decent physical existence, are preparations that men may be born from above.[11]

Laws that reduced labor hours, provided for common ownership of property, protected natural resources, and prohibited child labor—these were the means for "mothering" God. Such policies implemented on behalf of society would free individuals to live in greater fellowship with each other and God.

"New Womanhood"

An underlying theme in Scudder's understanding of human nature is the distinctive connection that she makes between women's creation in the image of God and their participation in God's redemptive acts. God's attributes are consistent in her writings with those that society identifies as feminine. This connection was natural for Scudder if for no other reason than her association with groups that were predominately composed of women. It also suggested her interest in freeing women to live into an image beyond that which society designed for them. Scudder's "new woman" would play an integral role in bringing about radical social change.

Gary Dorrien recently commented that Scudder's "interest in feminism paled next to her absorbing concerns."[12] It is true that Scudder did not enjoy "segregated discussions of women as women,"[13] but she never separated the need for social change from the need to increase the sphere of women's public influence. Women were not only to act as reformers; their activities and associations were also to serve as models for reform movements.

St. Catherine, a woman, embodied the type of behavior that Scudder called modern women to emulate. As one of the few pioneers in history who exited her domestic seclusion to work for social and political betterment, St. Catherine was characterized by Scudder as the patron of modern women. Like St. Francis, she lived in solidarity with the poor and ardently worked to reform the Church:

> From her youth of interior preparation, in that dyer's house where she was one of twenty-five children, she emerged into what we call the social services; healing the plague-stricken, ministering to prisoners, reconciling petty feuds in her native town. We see her gradually called to larger activities in the most important phases of civic and international life.[14]

Modern women shared a similar sequence in their lives as they began to move outside of their homes to activities in the public sphere.

Catherine was one of the greatest women in history, not because she always diagnosed social ailments correctly, but because she "bore those needs on her heart." Her interests centered on passionate devotion to God's Church, and she tried to apply Jesus' principles for living to the most difficult social issues of her day. Scudder discussed her relationship to Catherine and her disciples, the "Famiglia," in terms of an intimate friendship. Her friendship with this varied group helped her work out her own thought regarding adherence to institutional religion. The worldliness and corruption apparent in the Church itself threatened to sabotage Catherine's loyalty to her cause. Corruption shocked and agonized Catherine, but it remained clear to her that the Church also challenged materialism on a level unparalleled by other institutions. Failures at reform were unable to shake Catherine's loyalty because she did not seek reality through positive assurance. "No one more perfectly presents the perpetual paradox, supernatural life fostered and triumphantly revealed through a Church which too often crucifies the holy ones to whom it gives birth."[15]

Scudder understood the essential activity of human beings in relation to experiences common to women. That is not to say, however, that we can think of what she was doing in her time as constructing a totally new vision of women's leadership. Her arguments served to transfer women's private domain into the public sphere. For example, in her discussion of women's leadership in the home, Scudder directly linked cooperation to women's nature. The model for the Socialist State was the "mother state"; the "mother state" was a vision for a new social order that would transform "society from the likeness of a battlefield to the likeness of a home."[16] In Scudder's mind, however, her understanding of God's being as a social being and model for cooperative behavior undergirded her idea of state as mother. She viewed God's activity in feminine terms. Most certainly, her comparison of God's nature to women's nature pressed against dominant social and ecclesial traditions at the time. God's image, as Scudder understood it through God's cooperative behavior and egalitarian practices, was reflected in the activities and communities peculiar to women. Although Scudder did not radically reinterpret the concept of womanhood itself, she clearly argued that rethinking women's roles was a vital part of social change, and that women's contributions to the new social order should be highly valued and considered most significant.

Scudder wanted people to give special consideration to women's cooperative leadership, but she did not think that women were genetically predisposed to be more cooperative than their male counterparts. Resonating with Browning's modern interpretation of women's nature, she agreed that women did not differ from men: they had neither "peculiar goodness nor peculiar simplicity to set them in a class apart."[17] By limiting women's sphere of influence to the home, society stunted women's intellectual development,

Scudder thought. Women were "complex, subtle, involved"[18] and could not be understood in simple terms:

> They are not only gentle, silent influences, subduing by their very existence the passions and doubts of men; nor the victims, themselves unmoved, of the storms of fate. They are effective agents in bringing about the catastrophe of the drama. Great forces no longer pass over them and leave them unchanged or crushed; they become the protagonists of the struggle wherein the essence of dramatic art is found.[19]

A cooperative God, in whose image women were created, persuaded modern women to leave the seclusion of their homes and to enter society, confident that they could positively impact a social order greatly in need of change.

F. D. Maurice's Theology and Scudder's View of Human Nature

Harriet Scudder, Vida's mother, had been strongly influenced by F. D. Maurice, and she passed on an appreciation of his work to her daughter. Maurice attributed the social breakdown in England during the industrial revolution to a theological breakdown. He formulated his theological anthropology in response to the individualism emphasized by the early-nineteenth-century Evangelicalism that dominated English Protestantism. F. D. Maurice's theology informed Scudder's view of human nature.

Maurice argued that English Protestants wrongly oriented the discussion of human nature around the total depravity of humanity, God's vengeance against sinners. On the other hand, he understood human nature with reference to God's love for all humankind. For Maurice, sin "is defined as self-willed isolation from the true constitution of humankind as created and redeemed by Christ. Sin is the refusal to acknowledge our true center in Christ and the desperate effort to establish a false independence."[20]

In a letter to his fiancée, Miss Georgina Frances Hare, Maurice expressed his concern about the human moral condition. Human beings failed to recognize Christ as the "ground of all."[21] Their importance in history as God's instruments was understood more clearly in light of the gospel. According to Maurice, the incarnation revealed that God was within all of humanity. God's son "is *in* us. . . . The Gospel is, Christ with you and in you and He is in me."[22] All human beings, therefore, had the potential to act in obedience to God and to see beyond their own limitations and failures.

Although Scudder was hard-pressed to discuss her views of human failure in terms of sin, her assessment of the moral character nurtured by competitive capitalism exposed her social understanding of sin. She identified society's attitude of "defiant self-protection" as sinful because she was aware of God's contrary vision for a society ruled by fellowship, not self-seeking:

> We belong on our knees confessing our wrongdoing . . . because it is quite obvious that the sudden catastrophe in the Old World only revealed the latent evil everywhere. The normal tissue of our national American life has not been woven by Christianity. Our economic order is the natural outcome of forces with which religion has nothing whatever to do.[23]

Capitalism nurtured the progress of the sin of selfishness and self-interest as opposed to God's cooperative ideal.

Influenced by Maurice's view of human nature, Scudder understood human potential and failure in light of the incarnation. She defined sin as action contrary to God's real intentions for human community. Scudder agreed with Maurice that God was incarnate within all human beings. Redemption was not limited to Jesus' death on the cross, but rather extended to all human activity that focused on laboring to birth God's reality in the world. God created human beings to live in relationship with society and take part in redeeming it by engaging in activities patterned after Christ's suffering and sacrifice for the sake of others. Superimposing God's vision on top of social reality revealed where society missed the mark. It also revealed human potential to overcome social failures. This theological anthropology explained Scudder's focus on humanity's potential to realize God's social aims. Like other Social Gospelers, she was optimistic about the ability of human beings to correct their reprehensible mistakes. By creating the right social environment, individuals and institutions could move toward a more just society, in which they could foster their consciousness of God and social conscience.

Scudder departed from Maurice's line of thought by allowing her economic analysis to inform her social analysis. Maurice's thought was not economic, and he had little interest in social revolution. He never aimed to implement a radical program for social change. His interpretation of Christian socialism did not resemble modern, post-Marxist varieties.[24] Focusing on reform of society rather than revolution, Maurice objected to the competitive spirit encouraged in the new political economy on the grounds of its "selfish principle."[25] But he opposed trade unionism and looked to solve the problem by making "men fellow-workers instead of rivals,"[26] through the creation of brotherhoods that resonated the ideal of medieval guilds.

Scudder differed from Maurice in that she used scientific materialism to explore the alternative reality that society had chosen. Although she criticized socialists for their emphasis on human creativity, socialist doctrines revealed the extent to which the competitive capitalist social order based its decisions upon the potential for monetary gain. Scientific materialism raised society's consciousness of the plight of the working class. Integrating her cooperative and economic thought enabled Scudder to envision a more radical program for social change.

Clearly, Scudder understood human beings to be social by nature. Bringing this view of human nature into conversation with her diagnosis of an overly individualistic society persuaded Scudder to look for ways to attain a higher degree of fellowship. For human beings to live into their true nature of fellowship, they had to attain a greater degree of social justice. Beyond fellowship in human society, Scudder considered the extent to which a more just society would enable individuals to reach beyond themselves and strengthen their relationship with God.

Communities That Embodied God's Cooperative Image

There were some instances in which Scudder saw a glimpse of the social instinct breaking through the facade of individualism that seduced her society. Communities that approximated equality and cooperation encouraged individuals to live in fellowship with one another and freed them to focus on their relationship with God. The Franciscan brotherhood modeled the best of humanity's social instinct. Brother John, the protagonist of her historical novel about the first Franciscans, lived in loving community with his brothers and enjoyed communion with God. He attained the highest dignities of freedom. In some instances, the home encouraged cooperation among family members. Society had deprived women of their public role, but in the home they managed a microcosm of society that required cooperation. Women considered the needs of the whole family above individual needs of family members or their own personal needs.

The Society of Companions of the Holy Cross (SCHC) provided the best example of an organization that within its environs approximated God's vision for an egalitarian and cooperative society. The group was formed in the early 1880s in response to the needs of Adelyn Howard. Howard, at that time bedridden due to illness, had expressed to her friend Emily Malbone Morgan her desire to pray for a wider circle of people and her need for spiritual companionship. Morgan envisioned a group of women acting as "Companions of the Cross" by praying together on behalf of social causes.

They began sharing concerns by circulating a prayer list. As the Society grew, it became both contemplative and communal; its purpose was to cultivate the individual spirituality of its members and through prayer to work for social change. In 1914, the women designed and built Adelynrood, a summer retreat center frequented by the Companions. While in residence at Adelynrood, women gained a sense of spiritual autonomy and expressed their social concerns in friendly community.

Scudder joined the SCHC in 1889. She found that a sisterhood of Christian women not cloistered or bound by vows of poverty enabled her to bring together her concern for the social order and her interest in spirituality. Quoting Douglas Steere in a letter to one of her companions, Scudder stressed the important needs that the SCHC filled within American society: "A great need in our would-be democratic day is for Religious Orders which shall not bind their members to living together or to any form of corporate work, but shall be founded on unity of interior vocation, with membership diffused through secular society at large."[27] Through the SCHC these companions extended their sphere of influence beyond their individual homes and inward spiritual advancement to the communities in which they lived and actively participated.

Serving as the Companion-in-Charge of Probationers from 1907 to 1942, Scudder acted as a spiritual guide for women considering their call to be part of the SCHC. She signed her letters to the Probationers under her guidance as "Mother Vida" and took a real interest in their lives and spiritual journeys. Friendships with these women penetrated beneath a level of casual acquaintance. On many occasions companions visited Scudder at her home in Wellesley for brief or extended stays. They were devoted to one another through their devotion to following the way of the cross.

The leadership that Scudder provided in the SCHC was highly regarded by other Anglicans. She had been an inspiration to the founders of the Community of the Way of the Cross. In 1939, she was asked to become a Foundress for the Community. One of the followers of the Way of the Cross wrote, "Each time she has inspired, challenged, and fortified us by the clarity of her vision, the fire of her zeal, and the steadiness of her will for the bringing into being of 'a new heaven and a new earth,' wherein dwelleth righteousness."[28] Scudder declined their invitation because of her advanced age but thought it a worthy cause. The Community of the Way of the Cross honored her by dedicating the library in their Mother House to "Vida D. Scudder, Prophetess."

Martha Boonin-Vail pointed out that the SCHC made significant advances in cultivating women's leadership in the Anglican Church. Boonin-Vail regarded the Companions as successful in part because of their rejection of "male imagery of power and the hegemony of a male clergy."[29] They made their own decisions about worship, leadership, and property, and designed Adelynrood out of a feeling that "no male architect would know how to build to their needs."[30]

While the Companions did enjoy some sense of "spiritual autonomy" as women, Boonin-Vail's wording was a bit too strong with regard to their rejection of male leadership and imagery of power. Scudder herself suggested that the SCHC become a lay order of St. Francis.[31] Chaplains for the SCHC were exclusively male at the time that Scudder was a member, and many of the Companions enjoyed friendships with the ordained leadership of their Church. They were not of a single mind on such matters, and Scudder greatly appreciated this diversity of beliefs among them, as she said in writing to a Probationer:

> Some of us like myself are so far Left in politics that we might shock you (I wonder what your own affiliations are by the way)—others are quite at the other extreme—But we can all unite our prayers for social justice, and to learn unity in prayer is really a discipline which helps the larger unity which we all desire.[32]

To Scudder, diversity of opinions was a mark of real democracy.

Exercising their freedom to make decisions for themselves enabled Scudder to see the SCHC as encouraging the development of the "New Woman," one who was both professional and religious. The cooperation and spiritual advance of this sisterhood influenced Scudder's understanding of God and humanity, particularly her understanding of the unique ways in which women reflected God's image. It also certainly helped clear the way for her to argue that society ought to affirm the responsibility of women for the social order.

Jesus and St. Francis: Embodied Equality, Self-Sacrifice, and Solidarity

Scudder appealed to social solidarity, self-sacrifice, and equality as the means of achieving justice within the social setting. Following these norms and guidelines for moral action would lead to the kind of freedom and love known in Divine Society. The cooperative state would enable members of society to experience greater freedom, real religious freedom, and love. In making these appeals, she kept in mind the stories of certain figures that exemplified these norms.

The central principles that animated Jesus' and St. Francis's lives and teachings transcended their particular historical contexts; drawing upon their examples, Scudder felt confident that human beings could develop into better moral agents. Using Jesus and St. Francis as prominent sources for moral norms, Scudder understood such norms in light of her quest for the Cooperative Commonwealth. Jesus and St. Francis treated others as equals, sacrificed their own needs for the sake of community, drew upon their own relationship with God as a resource for daily living, and worked in solidarity with the poor. By following these norms as guidelines for daily living, they experienced true religious freedom and union with the infinite love known only in fellowship with God and among the human family.

Jesus' Embodiment of Key Values

Scudder linked equality to the equal distribution of wealth disbursed on the basis of need rather than for the fulfillment of services. Once freed from worry about material achievement, society could come closer to eliminating discrimination on the basis of race, class, and gender. An exemplar of the kind of behavior that would enable society to move toward greater equality, Jesus chose to live by a law contrary to prevailing social practices.

In his behavior Jesus embodied equality, solidarity, and self-sacrifice. "In perfect non-resistance, in gentlest love, He conspicuously preached and lived by laws which would have undermined the whole structure of civilization had all men embraced them."[33] Jesus espoused a social conception of the kingdom of God that emphasized the relationship between the inward journey of faith and its outward expression. Christ translated the interest in the value of life from the outward product to the inward sphere. His vision for the kingdom found in the Beatitudes reversed the general value system of his day as he offered blessings to the poor, hungry, and meek. His words tested human conduct rather than providing a place of quiet withdrawal for Christians. Like the prophets, Jesus connected God's kingdom with a reign of justice and equality:

> Jesus, even when most poetic, is never sentimental. If he presented the life of birds and flowers as the true model for human existence, it is because he actually believed that their freedom from anxious self-consciousness and their peaceful fulfillment of function were conditions that ought to be reproduced in economic relations.[34]

Living in solidarity with the poor, Jesus did not allow worry about material success to consume his thoughts and activities. Rather, he focused his energies on God's movement in the world. Reflecting upon the meaning of the Lord's Prayer, Scudder underscored Jesus' humility and concentration on discovering the nature of God within him and in his activities. Petitioning for God's kingdom to come on earth underscored the real inspiration behind all human progress. These words, however, did not make human beings "immune from action. The implied summons to it is imperious. But what wisdom, in the sequence of the aspirations from which our actions must proceed!"[35]

Jesus modeled sacrificing oneself for the greater good of the community. Instead of choosing to concern himself with personal comfort, he chose to participate in God's redemption. He did more than just sympathize with the oppressed; he became one of them. By sacrificing for the sake of others, Jesus showed the kind of love that God created for the social order and revealed God's interdependence with the world.

Echoing poet Walt Whitman's sentiments, Scudder characterized the kind of love that Christ called Christians to emulate: "I do not ask the wounded person how he feels; I myself become the wounded person."[36] Jesus' suffering revealed the nature of God that humanity was to reproduce. Christians had the same freedom to follow Christ and pick up the cross in a world full of suffering and defeat. By taking the way of the cross, Christians could place themselves under the influence of God's all-encompassing love. Recognizing themselves within God's sphere of influence enabled them to challenge any societal values that contradicted God's love. Succinctly put, "Following [Jesus]—that is the point. It is always the point. It must bring us as it brought Him to an attitude which will alienate and anger all the powers of this world."[37]

St. Francis Lived the Way of the Cross

Somewhat similarly, St. Francis lived the way of the cross by choosing to live in solidarity with the poor and teaching his followers to do the same. His concern was not for individual rights but for all to know the free grace of God. Two of Scudder's most cherished books, *Brother John* and *The Franciscan Adventure*, recorded the history of Franciscan communities. After her retirement from Wellesley in 1927, her study of Francis "became a sharp-pointed instrument of inquiry into the whole relation of Christianity to the ethics of private ownership."[38]

Scudder's interest in a Christian argument concerning private ownership caused her to dwell not only on Francis's relevance for modern life, but also on the history of the Franciscan movement. Francis renounced his own rights in the service of communal good. Scudder surmised, "The impelling inherited by his disciples was not the ascetic distrust of natural good, . . . but what we now call social compunction."[39] On the surface history would show the Franciscan experiment to be a failure, but both defeat and victory had been patent in Francis's own life:

> He died frustrated, cruelly wounded in the house of his friends, relentlessly foiled at every turn in his effort to realize his ideal. He died stigmatized. Yet triumphant; for he had gazed on the Seraph Crucified, on Love helpless, yet encircled and upborne by wings of power.[40]

The mendicant orders shared the irony of Francis's experiences. Scudder thought of the history of the orders as the most "ironic and picturesque example . . . of idealism pitted against a practical and proprietary world."[41] Enduring compromise after compromise, the Franciscan Order eventually defeated the effort to dispense with private property.

One would think that their inability to reach some sort of perfection under Francis's able guidance would have alienated Scudder. However, she avoided remembering their story only as one of disillusionment. Her intimacy with Francis and his followers destroyed two conservative assumptions held sacred by competitive society. First, the Franciscans proved that personality did not demand private property for its self-realization. Second, they disproved the idea that hope of gain was a necessary motivator for individual activity toward social progress. These men swam against the flow of the social systems of their day. They never separated themselves from the common life. They renounced property, individual or collective, and ignored what Scudder called "measurings of justice."[42] Tossing aside everything that was said to conserve society, they became "possessed by a paradoxical zeal for poverty."[43]

Believing themselves committed to Christ's imperative not to obsess about the material security of tomorrow, the brothers found a new perspective on life. In this new life, voluntary poverty and labor for the good of the community were the means of releasing love and creativity. Scudder characterized the life Brother John had found as a Franciscan monk:

> John found that his impulse to renounce the world had led him, not to a solitude but to a society. And what a society! Developing a life all its own, possessing its urgent questions, its struggles and incertitudes; a new

> civilization, penetrating the old dry social structure with strange and disturbing forces.[44]

The new life unlocked a creative power within them and consequently stimulated growth and prosperity within their society.

Scudder thought Francis's values were relevant to the modern situation and instructive for modern social reformers. Francis and his community bore witness to the notion that the rejection of private ownership was the gateway to freedom. Franciscan communities completely severed the connection between work and reward. They did not base reward for work upon merit but upon the needs of individuals as determined by the minimum of livelihood. In the Order, Francis maintained a tension between authority and freedom. Obedience to God was a virtue second only to poverty. Francis feared the development of intellectual values. His attitude toward intellectual development challenged Scudder because of her own commitment to education, but she carefully regarded his concern when learning that Franciscan Houses had introduced servants so that the brothers would have more time for study and prayer. These values were a guide for the social and political alignments of modern Christians.

The Franciscans' mistake had been their inability to think in economic terms. Nonetheless, their willingness to depart from society's conventions presented society with a sobering challenge. Admittedly, the global context had changed dramatically since Francis roamed the countryside of Umbria, but his sense of the relationship of individuals to the Whole would allow his theories to have bearing on the modern situation.

What Jesus and St. Francis had in common was that as human beings they entered into the process of redeeming society. They directed their moral thought and action toward the activity of God seen in the Trinity. Most important, Scudder did not emphasize their asceticism as a model for daily living; she emphasized the social passion that their spiritual devotion awakened. While she sometimes commented on the fact that she lived in relative comfort, she was also deeply engaged in working for change in society. The saints reminded her that God challenged her to think beyond her own needs.

Cooperative Commonwealth: Scudder's Loyalty

Society could more closely approximate God's justice if it fashioned itself in God's cooperative image; therefore, Scudder's ultimate loyalty was to building a truly Cooperative Commonwealth. Loyalty to the Cooperative Commonwealth gained support from Scudder's reading of humans as social beings. She understood a commitment to the common welfare as part of the nature of a people created in God's cooperative image. Such a commitment encompassed the values of justice, self-sacrifice, and equality.

As supported by her understanding of the good of humanity and humanity's relationship with God, the Cooperative Commonwealth was also the cause that lay behind her attitude toward social change. Her loyalty received decisive support from her understanding of God's Trinitarian nature. God's very being was social, cooperative, and egalitarian. And it was this concept of God that provided the basic orientation of her theology and informed her social ethic.

The interaction of key elements—Scudder's interpretation of the social circumstances, anthropological assumptions, loyalties, and values—built a case for her orientation toward social reform. Class antagonism, contrasting ethical practices for varying social classes, and valuing individuals on the basis of their contribution to the means of production—all these indicated that society had compromised and even threatened God's vision of society. The assumptions that people could grab hold of their own social destinies and bring society into greater harmony with the rhythm that God intended for it encouraged Scudder to believe that people could significantly improve the present social situation. Scudder's understanding of the value of self-sacrifice, social solidarity, and equality as a means toward love and freedom represented a commitment to human fellowship; such characteristics gathered support from the presupposition that humans are inherently social. When brought to bear on society and considered in light of the knowledge that human beings are also shaped by their social conditions, these values encouraged Scudder to think that something was very wrong with society and that drastic action was necessary.

Policies for a Cooperative Commonwealth

Walter Rauschenbusch spoke about his program for social change in terms of "Christianizing" the social order; Scudder's program might be best described as transforming the social order in light of God's cooperative image. She thought that socialist policies informed by Christian principles would be most likely to accomplish this goal. Christianity was best suited for the socialist state because of its historic character, but she did not think that any one religion would maintain dominance over another in the ideal social setting. Scudder questioned the value of private property as a means to promote the common good. For her, collective ownership of property was the means to achieve religious or spiritual freedom. In the Cooperative Commonwealth, communal needs would supersede the needs of individuals.

Labor Regulation

Great variation existed among socialist arguments for specific policies that would implement a vision of common ownership of government and the means of production. Scudder argued that society could achieve cooperation through the voluntary renunciation of private property in order to serve the common good. Placing the community in charge of decisions regarding laws that affected laborers would free individuals to focus on their relationship with God. Average workers would then be included in decision-making done on their behalf. In her mind, cooperative decision-making would yield fairer laws, which would favor the common good above individual progress. She did not argue for uniformity in compensation for work or distribution of property; workers in the Cooperative Commonwealth would have the opportunity to raise their earnings if they chose to do so. Society would not measure compensation and distribution in terms of an individual's contribution to production but to each according to need. Industry would be obligated to pay enough wages to maintain men and women in a standard necessary for them to live in decency and health.[45] Her intent was to establish laws that valued the well-being and mind of each individual as a member of a larger society.

When giving her controversial speech to the strikers at Lawrence in 1912, she spoke out for workers in the woolen industry, displaying great passion in calling for justice:

> I speak for thousands besides myself when I say that I would rather never again wear a thread of woolen than know that my garments had been woven at the cost of such misery as I have seen and known, past the shadow of a doubt, to have existed in this town.[46]

She came out in support of a minimum wage in Massachusetts and "reasonable profits"[47] for stockholders and manufacturers in the industry.

In *Socialism and Character*, Scudder admitted that her personal vision often lacked the necessary practical provisions for its implementation. It is helpful to further explore her preferences for public policy with reference to the platform of the Socialist Labor Party in the United States. Socialists made a variety of social demands that would return to the working class power that industrialists had usurped. Their demands included the reduction of the hours of labor, provisions to protect workers from being discharged for political reasons, the incorporation of local trade unions in the states that had no national organization, the regulation of child care and female labor, proper consideration for the health and well-being of all employees, and provision of proper sanitary facilities for all workers. In addition to these labor policies, socialists argued for the public ownership of telegraphs, telephones, railroads, and all other means of transportation, and that provisions be made for the public ownership of green spaces in overcrowded cities.

Scudder aligned herself with groups intent on changing society rather than reforming it. Richard Ely and Rauschenbusch advocated for similar reforms, though in some instances less radical ones. Ely urged reformers to focus on proactive legislation that would guide social evolution. He valued socialist methodology because it exposed the problems of the current social system, but he thought that Marx incorrectly assessed the outcome of the social situation. One could cite examples where society had proactively addressed the social problem. Earlier socialistic legislation in England called for the regulation of mines and merchant shipping, the inspection of factories and workshops, the Truck Act, the Artisans' Dwellings Act, the Allotments Act, the Education Act, the Poor Law, and the Irish Land Acts.[48] General Booth had been right to speak about the "submerged tenth" in *Darkest England*, but Ely pointed out that nine-tenths of the population was not immersed in poverty. Social reformers had to strive to accomplish three things: the reduction of the waste of a competitive system to its lowest possible terms; the distribution of wealth to avoid extremes and attain comfort among all people; and the cultivation of abundant public provisions for opportunities that would develop individual faculties such as educational facilities and widespread use of natural resources for recreation.[49]

Calling for the "Christianization" of everyday life, Rauschenbusch argued for political and religious influences to cooperate in an effort to challenge the political economy to put "man before wealth."[50] He saw Christianity as based on equality and translated into society as economic and political equality. Rauschenbusch supported reforms that would guard against the exploitation of children, counteract the tendency of tenement owners to crowd housing under their management, limit the working day to eight hours, and require breaks for workers. Finding value in society's communistic organizations, he affirmed the value of public schools, public parks, and the public ownership of utilities as instruments that would benefit the health of the working class.[51]

Suffrage for Women a Duty, Not a Right

The social demands of the Socialist Labor Party were matched by a set of political demands showing their intent to reorganize the political power structure of the nation. They demanded the right of common people to propose laws and vote upon all measures of importance, the abolition of all privileges of executive veto, municipal self-government, and the abolition of capital punishment. Perhaps the most striking petition was for the universal and equal right of suffrage for all people, regardless of their race, creed, or gender.[52] James Weinstein declared that no "other political party or organization embodied the social values of various women's rights organizations as did the Socialist Party; no other group fought consistently for the full enfranchisement of women."[53]

Not all Socialists favored suffrage, but the women's right to vote was the main concern of the Women's Committee in the Party and was part of the Party's general platform. In states where suffrage was denied, Socialists campaigned for its adoption. In states that elected Socialist legislators, the Party introduced pro-suffrage resolutions. Between 1907 and 1913 these legislators introduced seven such resolutions in various states. Socialists also played a significant role in the suffrage campaigns advanced in at least three states: Nevada, Kansas, and New York. In sum, "wherever the Socialist propaganda made headway, the suffrage vote automatically increased."[54]

Directly linked to Scudder's concern for policies that would ensure fair and equal treatment of the working class was the cause of woman suffrage. In line with Socialist demands for universal suffrage, she supported women's right to vote because she thought of it as a "duty, not a right."[55] In increasing numbers lower-class women had entered the factories as common laborers. Society had begun to confront questions concerning what to do with women working outside the home. By hiring servants, middle-class women had been freed from many domestic duties. Time away from household chores enabled them to consider social responsibilities beyond their families. From Scudder's perspective, the economic emancipation of women would liberate society from the grip of sexism, classism, and racism.

Scudder, however, did not align herself directly with organizations working specifically for suffrage causes. Teresa Corcoran said that Scudder was dissatisfied with the prejudices espoused by many suffragists.[56] Scudder never approved of women using the ballot to protect their own private interests. Although she met Julia Ward Howe when she visited Denison House and described that meeting as a "happy occasion,"[57] she set herself apart from other feminists and focused on the broader issue of rallying people to work toward the genesis of a new social system. The new society that she envisioned would value the contributions of women and men, regardless of class or race, in both the private and public domains, and women would have a significant role to play in the public sphere.

References to the "woman movement" consistently appeared in the writings of Social Gospelers, but they never seemed to achieve consensus on the issue of "the woman movement." Unable to emerge totally from the shadow of Victorian attitudes toward women, Social Gospelers disagreed about how women could continue to nurture the family while working outside the home. Jane Addams argued that the only way a modern woman could properly manage the household was by being able to vote. Realizing that the public domain influenced the private aspects of all individuals' lives, Addams became a well-known advocate for women's right to vote:

> Many women today are failing to discharge their duties to their own households properly because they do not perceive that as society grows more complicated it is necessary that women shall extend her sense of responsibility to many things outside of her own home if she would continue to preserve the home in its entirety.[58]

Women needed to be able to vote in order to impact decisions concerning sanitary conditions for their homes and the education of their children.

Susan Lindley thought that "few (male) Social Gospel leaders supported women's suffrage in the nineteenth century, but neither were they among the most conservative forces who insisted on woman's full submission and silence."[59] Charles Stelzle was more sympathetic of the need to include women in the struggle for social justice. He made significant "efforts to reach and organize women and blacks in the cause of social Christianity."[60] In a letter stating his opinion on suffrage, Rauschenbusch admitted that he "sat on the top rail of the fence about suffrage for about twenty years."[61] When he finally decided to support suffrage, he thought that women would make a good contribution to the public domain,[62] but he was not fond of the suffragist's tactics. In the same letter he likened Emmaline Pankhurst to a panther. Unlike Addams, he did not underscore female virtuosity in favoring suffrage. For Rauschenbusch, women's right to vote was a practical matter:

> I finally decided for suffrage at the time of the shirtwaist strike in New York. The decisive consideration was not the need of the intellectual women, but of the industrial workers. If they are to go out of the family into industrial life and fight their economic battle on the same terms as men, they need the same weapons. The suffrage is fundamentally a weapon of protection and sometimes of offence.[63]

From Pacifism of the Future to Pacifism as Resistance

World War One raised new and challenging questions regarding the nation's policies for the use of violence and the relationship of women to the war machine. Social reformers began more systematically to connect their social concerns with their attitudes toward world peace. Scudder chose not to "add much to the all-too-voluminous literature"[64] about the war. Early in her career, the indignation that Scudder felt at the mistreatment of the working class caused her to support the use of force in an effort to alleviate their suffering. As World War Two appeared to be imminent, she expressed her regret that she had not considered Jane Addams's position that war only created more problems than it solved, and Scudder took a pacifist stance. She concluded that war was the most extreme form of competition in society.

Remembering her feelings in reaction to the outbreak of the war in August 1914 Scudder wrote:

> Somehow it seemed that I had always expected something like this, almost desired it. My repulsion from modern civilization had been intense, though still. I felt the social order in which we moved to be poisoned at the roots, beneath its smooth suave surface. And my sad impatience, which smoldered and burned in the depths of my consciousness, experienced a terrible sensation something like relief, when the great explosion came.[65]

Perhaps the war would purge the world of its self-centered rottenness. During the years that preceded World War One, Scudder stood for what she called a kind of pacifism of the future.

When a reporter for *The Intercollegiate Socialist* asked about how she thought Socialists should view the war, Scudder said that they "should in general be in the front ranks of pacifism, but I am not prepared to take the extreme position that force is never justifiable in international relationships."[66] "War of chivalry" waged by the strong on behalf of the weak and "defensive war" when a country is invaded by another is justifiable. We should regard these solutions to international problems, however, as last resorts. Socialists should focus on more constructive measures even during wartime by encouraging free speech, global awareness, the adoption of socialistic measures by all countries, and the insistence on renunciation of wealth by the "propertied classes."[67]

In her article entitled "The Doubting Pacifist," Scudder argued that the real lovers of peace looked to solve the social problems that contributed to war, but we might deem war necessary in working toward eventual peace. Pacifism equated the suppression of war with peace, but for Scudder, "the suppression of war is not the equivalent of peace."[68] Modern society had submerged a large group of people for whom living in peace had become impossible. They could not escape the strikes, the class war, the race war, and the slums. For these people, war could come as a relief.

Scudder thought it possible to kill and to love, but only for the right reasons. Some absolute pacifists had argued against war on the basis that "the taking of human life is the supreme wrong because it destroys the supreme sanctity—personality."[69] For her, this line of reasoning did not provide an adequate basis to avoid war. "The flesh is at best only the outward and visible sign in the sacrament of personality, and over-emphasis on the outward sign is always dangerous."[70] Using a story from the Bhagavad Gita to further explain her position, Scudder suggested that Christians and Hindus shared a common understanding that "physical death is an episode in life and not the end of life."[71] The agonies inflicted by war were not reason enough to end war. Christians believed that God shared in human suffering; "to shrink from suffering per se were to abandon the adoration of the One crucified."[72]

Bernard Markwell suggested that Scudder's rejection of absolute pacifism at this point in her career "anticipates the searching comments of Reinhold Niebuhr."[73] Committed to a "troubled pacifism" following World War One, Niebuhr shifted his opinion toward the use of force to bring about social change. By 1932 Niebuhr recognized his own discomfort with pacifism. At this point in history, he could no longer consider pacifism as an option for a person endeavoring to be politically responsible. His use of Marxist analysis of social ills served only to bring the issue of coercion more sharply into focus. For a person concerned with the plight of the socially disinherited and the struggle for equality, he decided, a position for absolute pacifism had clearly become untenable.

Markwell thought that Scudder's view of the cross as both divine judgment and symbol of social innovation was the foundation for her "doubting pacifism." During these years she and Niebuhr shared the view that a world without justice would not experience peace. Later, however, Scudder became dissatisfied with this approach. She admitted that she regretted writing "The Doubting Pacifist," not because the article misrepresented her views at the time, but because she thought that it emphasized the wrong things for the moment.[74] Scudder confessed that she wished she had listened more intently to her friend Jane Addams on the subject of war. Addams had taken a pragmatic approach of opposition to war in her book *Newer Ideals of Peace*; she opposed war on the grounds that it was a wasteful and ineffective method of solving social problems. In sum, war created more problems than it solved.[75]

No Longer in Doubt

After the armistice ending World War One was signed, many Americans realized that the war had not made the "world safe for democracy." Scudder increasingly realized that the war had the effect of preserving the status quo and the values of an economic system that she abhorred. In 1923, Scudder joined the Fellowship of Reconciliation as the group began to integrate its understanding of pacifism more and more with a commitment to drastic social reorganization.[76] Scudder began to see that her dual commitment to Marxist revolutionary ardor and longing for spiritual peace would not rest together comfortably. She had long identified the proletariat with a messianic function; but as she witnessed the events following the revolution in Russia, she concluded that the use of force could not found "brotherhood":

> But as coercion and cruelty were continuously impounded as means to reach justice and brotherhood, uncritical enthusiasm waned. Helped, as I shall presently tell, by Franciscan studies, I became increasingly convinced that no revolution could bring ultimate salvation unless it proceeded from a Christian conception of man.[77]

By the eve of World War Two, she had committed herself to pacifism. The means of war had proved futile in an effort to achieve peace. In "Foeman Vassals," she wrote that she detested the use of wrong methods to take a stand against the war. Absolute pacifism, she thought, carried with it a feeling of anti-Semitism. While she opposed these views, she urged pacifists to take a stand with the prophets and oppose war in an effort not to resort to the tactics used by the other side.

Opposing war meant opting out of competitive society. Where she had once renounced pacifism because she thought of war as a by-product of evil, she now saw pacifism as a stance against a problematic social system. Although it directly contradicted her faith, she was well aware that she had no choice but to live in competitive society; she even benefited from it. Scudder could not avoid eating food and consuming other goods produced by competitive society, but she could protest war in an effort to take a stand against society's most extreme level of competition.

Pacifists, she thought, needed to pay attention to "other forces at work," those that were "secret, silent, constructive."[78] She never supported active opposition to war during wartime. Rather, she persuaded pacifists to invest their energies in work that encouraged cooperative society. Positive energies could be invested in

> agrarian reform movements, Workers education, Quaker work camps, Catholic Worker Farm Communes, Ashrams sometimes with a practical core, cooperatives in China, Japan, Latin America, U.S.A. Here and, mirabile dictu, in England, an amazing number of small communal colonies trying to live the life of the economic future in the economic present appear like wee green patches in the contemporary Waste Land.[79]

Pacifists would find hope in a seemingly hopeless situation by choosing to live by the law of Christ. Christ's law limited national sovereignty, accepted the rights of workers in concerns related to employment, and invited all of humanity to yield their own will to power, voluntarily subjecting themselves to the common good. Pointing out her later differences of opinion with Reinhold Niebuhr, Scudder asserted that the cross was the central symbol of the pacifist's faith:

> He [the pacifist] can not see the Cross as Reinhold Niebuhr does, at the edge of history, a sad estray from eternity into the world of time. Rather it is to him the very centre of history, the source of all abiding progress, the only banner under which Mercy and Truth can meet together, and Righteousness and Peace achieve their miraculous embrace.[80]

According to Niebuhr, those who opposed war on the basis that it violated the law of love showed their moral confusion. Their opposition meant that, in the name of love, injustice was preferred over the resistance necessary to gain a higher justice. Christian perfectionists correctly insisted that love was the ultimate law of life, but incorrectly assumed "that we have not right or duty to defend a civilization, despite its imperfections, against worst alternatives."[81] Niebuhr felt that their complacency fed the growing movement toward totalitarianism in Germany and other countries. Christ's atoning death had taught Christians about God's love and mercy, but we could not fully understand that love in historical terms. Rather, the cross revealed that the perfect love of God finally transcends all of history. The cross stood as a lure to humanity to reach toward God's aims and also as a reminder that human efforts to reach that goal would always fall short. For Niebuhr, it was clear that in certain instances coercion was necessary to approximate justice even though perfection could never be attained.

Scudder, however, disagreed. Following the law of Christ meant not only voluntarily renouncing worldly goods but also voluntarily renouncing worldly values. Nations had used war to bolster the very social system that entrapped the working class and the poor. Opting out of the cycle of violence would enable society to take steps toward a world organized according to cooperation rather than competition. She concluded that renouncing war put the way of love seen in the cross in control of a war-torn world.

During World War Two and the years following that war, Scudder committed herself to a pacifist agenda. She aligned herself with groups seeking to promote peaceful resolution to national and international conflicts, and she actively opposed discrimination against anyone on the basis of race, creed, or gender. Placed under surveillance in 1941 by the Federal Bureau of Investigation (FBI), the bureau observed Scudder's activities as part of the "C program," which identified and kept track of Communist sympathizers. The FBI kept a picture of Scudder on file "in case of national emergency."

Scudder held memberships in organizations deemed subversive by the House Committee of Un-American Activities, such as the Fellowship of Reconciliation; the National Council of Arts, Sciences and Professions; the Joint Anti-Fascist Refugee Committee; and the Progressive Citizens of America. The House Committee was particularly interested in Scudder's support of the National Council of American-Soviet Friendship, a group formed to work toward bringing an end to the Cold War and to finding a peaceful settlement of United States and Soviet disagreements.[82] Scudder remained highly suspect during the years that Senator Joseph McCarthy was in office because she donated money to relief efforts in Russia following World War Two and protested the unfair treatment of Communists on more than one occasion. An example of this was her endorsement of a petition in 1953 that appealed for clemency for eleven convicted Communist leaders.

A former member of the Communist Party, Louis Budenz, reported to FBI officers that she was a concealed Communist, "one who does not hold himself out as a Communist and who would deny membership in the party."[83] However, it is highly unlikely that Scudder maintained a concealed identity. She proudly claimed her membership in the Socialist Party but denied having an interest in joining the Communist Party in spite of her Communist sympathies.

Scudder adamantly opposed McCarthy and McCarthyism, and the violence and repression that it represented. Just six months before her death, she attended a conference of the New England Progressive Party in Boston. Motions made by the conference included calling for forty hours' pay for thirty hours' work, one hundred million dollars to be allocated by the government for food for the unemployed, extension of benefits to the unemployed, and a proposal that the unemployed be hired to build homes, roads, and other things. A petition also called for all representatives at the conference to support African-American candidates for political offices and those candidates for public office who opposed McCarthyism.[84]

Notes

1. Vida Dutton Scudder, *Social Teachings of the Christian Year* (New York: Dutton, 1921), 214.
2. Vida Dutton Scudder, *Socialism and Character* (London: Dent, 1912), 353.
3. Vida Dutton Scudder, *Christian Citizenship: Presented at the Triennial Meeting of the Woman's Auxiliary to the National Council, Atlantic City, New Jersey* (New York: Women's Auxiliary, 1934), 12.
4. Vida Dutton Scudder, *My Quest for Reality* (Wellesley, MA.: Printed for the author, 1952), 66–67.
5. See George Bernard Shaw, ed., *The Fabian Essays in Socialism* (1889; repr., London: George Allen & Unwin, 1950), 53.
6. Scudder, *Social Teachings of the Christian Year*, 52.
7. Ibid.
8. Ibid., 45.
9. Ibid., 53.
10. Ibid., 54.
11. Ibid., 53–54.
12. Gary Dorrien, *The Making of American Liberal Theology: Idealism, Realism, and Modernity* 1900–1950 (Louisville: Westminster John Knox Press, 2003), 128.

13. Vida Dutton Scudder, *On Journey* (New York: Dutton, 1937), 64.
14. Ibid., 243.
15. Ibid.
16. Vida Dutton Scudder, "Woman and Socialism," *The Yale Review* 3 (April 1914): 470.
17. Vida Dutton Scudder, "Womanhood in Modern Poetry," *Poet Lore* 1 (October 15, 1889): 458.
18. Ibid., 457.
19. Ibid., 458.
20. William J. Wolf, John E. Booty, and Owen C. Thomas, eds., *The Spirit of Anglicanism: Hooker, Maurice, Temple.* (Wilton, CT: Morehouse-Barlow, 1979), 81.
21. Frederick D. Maurice, *The Life of Frederick Denison Maurice* (vol. 1; New York: Charles Scribner's Sons, 1884), 508.
22. Ibid., 509–10.
23. Vida Dutton Scudder, "The Alleged Failure of the Church," *The Yale Review* 6 (January 1917): 327–28.
24. Wolf et al., *The Spirit of Anglicanism*, 63.
25. Edward Norman, *Church and Society in England, 1770–1970* (Oxford: Clarendon, 1976), 174.
26. Ibid.
27. Vida Dutton Scudder to Jessie Degen, August 19, 1949. Scudder files, Archives of the Society of Companions of the Holy Cross, Adelynrood, South Byfield, MA.
28. Author unknown, "Vida D. Scudder," *Work and Way* (October 1953). Clipping found in Scudder Files, Archives of the Society of Companions of the Holy Cross, Adelynrood, South Byfield, MA.
29. Martha Clara Boonin-Vail, "New Wine in Old Bottles" (PhD diss., Yale University, 1993), 233n102.
30. Ibid., 239.
31. Ibid., 235.
32. Vida Dutton Scudder to Hilda Munson, 1937, Scudder Files, Archives of the Society of Companions of the Holy Cross, Adelynrood, South Byfield, MA.
33. Vida Dutton Scudder, "The Last Beatitude," *The Witness* 7 (February 1923): 8.
34. Scudder, *Socialism and Character*, 267.
35. Scudder, *My Quest for Reality*, 98.
36. Vida Dutton Scudder, "Education for the New Day," *The World Tomorrow* 3 (December 1920): 10.
37. Scudder, "The Last Beatitude," 8.
38. Scudder, *On Journey*, 322.
39. Vida Dutton Scudder, "The Franciscan Adventure," *The Atlantic Monthly* 145 (June 1930): 808.
40. Scudder, *On Journey*, 322.
41. Ibid., 323.
42. Vida Dutton Scudder, "Franciscan Parallels," *Anglican Theological Review* 5 (March, 1923): 283.
43. Scudder, "The Franciscan Adventure," 811.
44. Vida Dutton Scudder, *Brother John: A Tale of the First Franciscans* (Boston: Little, Brown, 1927), 49.
45. "Miss Scudder's Criticized Speech: Just What She Said at a Citizens' Meeting in Lawrence, to Which Exception Has Been So Excitedly Taken by the Brahmins," *The Boston*

Common, March 9, 1912, 6–7. Clipping found in Scudder Papers, Wellesley College Archives, Margaret Clapp Library, Wellesley College, Wellesley, MA.

46. Ibid., 7.
47. Ibid., 6.
48. Richard Ely, *Socialism and Social Reform* (New York: Thomas Y. Crowell, 1894), 259.
49. Ibid., 256–57.
50. Walter Rauschenbusch, *Christianity and the Social Crisis* (1907; repr., Louisville: Westminster/John Knox Press, 1991), 371.
51. Ibid., 398.
52. Ely, *Socialism and Social Reform*, 378–79.
53. James Weinstein, *The Decline of Socialism in America, 1912–1925* (New York: Random House, 1967), 54.
54. Ibid., 61.
55. Vida Dutton Scudder, "The Educated Woman as a Social Factor: III," *The Christian Union* 35 (April 21, 1887): 12.
56. Teresa Corcoran, *Vida Dutton Scudder* (Boston: Twayne, 1982), 102.
57. Scudder, *On Journey*, 257.
58. Jane Addams, *The Social Thought of Jane Addams* (ed. Christopher Lasch; Indianapolis: Bobbs-Merrill, 1965), 144.
59. Susan Lindley, "*You Have Stept Out of Your Place: A History of Woman and Religion in America*" (Louisville: Westminster/John Knox Press, 1996), 136.
60. Paul T. Phillips, *A Kingdom on Earth: Anglo-American Social Christianity, 1880–1940* (University Park, PA: The Pennsylvania State University Press, 1996), 146.
61. Walter Rauschenbusch to Mrs. John W. Blodgett, April 19, 1913. Walter Rauschenbusch Papers, American Baptist Historical Society Manuscript Collection, Samuel Colgate Historical Library, Colgate Rochester Divinity School, Rochester, NY.
62. See Walter Rauschenbusch, "Is the Woman's Movement Going to Save Society?" *Ford Hall Folks* 2, no. 28 (April 26, 1914).
63. Walter Rauschenbusch to Mrs. John W. Blodgett, April 19, 1913.
64. Scudder, *On Journey*, 278.
65. Ibid., 279.
66. Vida Dutton Scudder, "Socialists and the Problem of War: A Symposium," *The Intercollegiate Socialist* 5 (April–May 1917): 20.
67. Ibid., 21.
68. Vida Dutton Scudder, "The Doubting Pacifist," *The Yale Review* 6 (July 1917): 738.
69. Ibid., 742.
70. Ibid.
71. Ibid., 743.
72. Ibid., 745.
73. Bernard K. Markwell, *The Anglican Left* (Brooklyn, NY: Carlson, 1991), 222.
74. Scudder, *On Journey*, 282.
75. Addams, *The Social Thought of Jane Addams*, 218.
76. Scudder, *On Journey*, 302.
77. Ibid., 306.
78. Vida Dutton Scudder, "Foeman Vassals: A Pacifist Apologia," *The Protestant* 4, no. 2 (October/November 1941): 50.
79. Ibid., 50.
80. Ibid., 51.

81. Reinhold Niebuhr, *Love and Justice: Selections from the Shorter Writings of Reinhold Niebuhr* (ed. D. B. Robertson; Philadelphia: Westminster, 1957), 280.

82. FBI Report of January 30, 1951, Scudder Files, Archives of the Society of Companions of the Holy Cross, Adelynrood, South Byfield, MA.

83. FBI Report of August 21, 1950, Scudder Files, Archives of the Society of Companions of the Holy Cross, Adelynrood, South Byfield, MA.

84. FBI Report of April 3, 1954, Scudder Files, Archives of the Society of Companions of the Holy Cross, Adelynrood, South Byfield, MA.

5
Scudder's Social Vision: An Enduring Legacy

Vida Dutton Scudder prepared the prelude to her memoirs while visiting the Uffizi Gallery in Florence, Italy. She reflected on her place within the pageant of Christian history:

> Does my little modern self . . . belong in this room with all these Holy Ones? Not with the Roman soldiers or in Nativity but with the crowds of little citizens in the background, onlookers merely, or, . . . just plain folk working in the fields busy with tasks or pleasures and quite unaware often of the marvels close at hand, and each life of supreme importance to itself; and supremely interesting to anyone with eyes to see. I propose to press in among them, insignificant as I am. . . . I am playing my own part in this world's redemption. . . . I am no onlooker, I am one of the actors.[1]

The Impact of Her Work

Through her writing, teaching, and activism, Scudder plunged deep into the world's troubled seas and challenged the complacency of Christians toward the world's affairs. She believed that others could judge the impact of her work when ideas were freed from the isolation of her mind and her readers discussed, questioned, and acted upon them. When Scudder was awarded an honorary Doctor of Letters from Smith College in 1922, William A. Neilson judged the impact of her writing and teaching to be distinguished. His tribute to her captured the breadth of her accomplishments and emphasized the religious beliefs that provided the foundation for her academic and reformist pursuits:

> Professor of English Literature in Wellesley College, an apostle of social justice, an international authority in religious biography, a skilled interpreter of English poetry, who has brought honor to her alma mater and invaluable service to the college of her adoption through her spiritual insight, her humanitarian zeal, and the contagious enthusiasm of her writing and teaching.[2]

The Living Church published an obituary in memory of her entitled "Far-Reaching Influence" and called her "one of the towering figures of her generation."[3] Emily Greene Balch—Scudder's dear friend, colleague in the Economics Department at Wellesley, and fellow Companion—remembered that Scudder was able to accomplish what others could not: she combined her love for the Church, its tradition and ritual, with her radical concern for a just, egalitarian social order.

Most often her books received favorable reviews. Readers warmly greeted *On Journey* and *Brother John*. Lois Hiesland called the autobiography "charming" and billed it as a "zestful account" of Scudder's life.[4] A reviewer of *Socialism and Character* applauded Scudder's ideas, though he found her writing style difficult.[5] One commentator on her work simply titled his review of Scudder's *On Journey* and Florence Converse's *Collected Poems*, "Vida Scudder and Florence Converse Write Fine Books."[6] However, in spite of the praise for her well-reasoned theories and passionate commitment, critics of her work most often questioned the theological basis for her investment in social change.

Even some of her fellow Companions in the Society of Companions of the Holy Cross hesitated to accept her ideas and the radical implications they had for their lives of faith. Emily Malbone Morgan, founder of the SCHC, and Scudder disagreed as to the manner in which the Companions should express their social concerns. Both Morgan and Scudder agreed that social justice was of preeminent concern for their prayers and private activism, but Morgan did not see public involvement in causes for reform part of the Companions' duties.[7] Sister Mary Theodora also thought Scudder was too preoccupied with material affairs.[8] Scudder appreciated their differences of opinion but remained the activist, and she urged her fellow Companions to see the issue of social justice as the unifying voice amid their theological diversity.

In many ways criticisms of Scudder's theological leanings validated her concern that the churchgoers of her generation often failed to link theological concepts with contemporary social issues. She complained that dominant theological trends rested too heavily on an inward spirituality and never culminated in outward action, in effect encouraging materialism. Churches that focused too much on an otherworldly spirituality had failed to teach about or empathize with the poor and the powerless. Their lack of concern for the oppression of the working class impacted society's treatment of them. Society herded the working poor into tenement houses, placed a high value on a "pull yourselves up by your bootstraps" ethic, and celebrated the achievements of the rich as endowed by God. Imprisoned by their social environment, the working class was unable to concentrate on anything but their lack of material resources, Scudder thought. In other words, the theological theories of recent generations implied a social theory of disregard for the oppressed.

Scudder's theology was closely tied to her social theory; however, this was the result of her understanding of God, not of materialism. Her worldview did not allow her to draw thick lines between the sacred and the secular. God was within the creation and within natural and worldly affairs; the universe depended upon both God and humanity for creativity, innovation, and survival. The cooperative relationship that existed between the three members of the Trinity provided the basis for Scudder's pursuit of an egalitarian society. God acted according to an egalitarian ethic and called those made in God's image to follow suit. God revealed Godself as concerned about human affairs, as loving others by sacrificing a part of Godself for the sake of others, and as a continual presence enlivening human beings to do the same.

God created human beings in that same cooperative image. Although Christians had interpreted their doctrine in a way that repressed the poor, the working class, and women, Scudder did not think that freedom from doctrine would necessarily mean freedom for the oppressed. Christian doctrine could provide the gateway to human liberation. The creeds gave Christians a clearer vision of God's liberating activity in the history of social action. Scudder offered examples of Christian communities that achieved some approximation of God's egalitarian vision. She affirmed the essential nature of women as a creation of God and emphasized women's potential to be agents for social change. Scudder did not radically redefine women's private roles, but she clearly defined their responsibility in the public forum. Women served as prototypes of moral behavior in the way that they modeled cooperation in the home and through their social service. Exceptional women such as St. Catherine of Siena challenged others to follow Christ's lead and address public concerns. Scudder affirmed the potential for women in their daily lives to interpret what it meant to live in a cooperative and egalitarian society.

For Scudder, cooperation and egalitarianism mean living in relationship, all people with differing needs, talents, and circumstances contributing to their common life in equal but diverse ways. Believing this, her faith was disposed toward action rather than a place of quiet withdrawal from the world. Through her discussion of the prevailing attitudes toward the working class, Scudder unmasked the materialism that stifled humanity; she aimed to free all Christians to pursue more genuine relationships with God and with others.

The reform movements with which Scudder was involved enjoyed varying degrees of success. She judged their accomplishments according to their aims to achieve better conditions for moral and spiritual growth. Underscoring the value of the settlement movement, she explained: "As Christians and good citizens, the residents try to help in bringing about better conditions materially, morally and spiritually in the community in which they live."[9]

Scudder emerged as an influential lay leader among Anglicans. In 1942 she received an honorary Doctorate of Divinity from Nashotah House. From its founding in 1842, the mission of Nashotah House was to prepare men and women for ministry in the Catholic tradition. Among other things, the seminary was committed to nurturing among its students active attention to contemporary social concerns in light of the gospel. Church leaders frequently wrote to her to thank her for her inspiring books and thought-provoking commentaries on how Christianity could address social needs. Randolph Ray, rector of Church of the Transfiguration in New York City, commended her for *Social Teachings of the Christian Year:* "Since its publication [it] has been a veritable handbook of mine. From it I have gained a great deal of inspiration. . . . I want to thank you for your books and tell you how very much I have enjoyed them."[10]

Through her teaching at Wellesley College, and in other contexts, Scudder played a significant role in preparing young women to act as leaders in the New World Order. She hoped to inspire her students to find within themselves the power to appreciate the right things. Her goal, she declared, was to "create the right people to live in the new and dawning day."[11] Scudder instilled within them the desire to be humble and to develop their passive and contemplative powers. Well-prepared leaders for a new society would draw upon their relationship with the God who modeled egalitarian and cooperative behavior for them. For Scudder, forty years of involvement in this social experiment was her greatest accomplishment because this was the adventure in social reform that had truly succeeded.[12]

Scudder's Enduring Legacy

In the years that followed World War One, Social Gospelers realized that many programs for reform were unable to reach the heights that they had once imagined. Others criticized the movement itself for being overly optimistic, sentimental, and moralistic. At times Social Gospelers failed to understand the complexity and systemic nature of social problems. For example, Rauschenbusch failed to make strong enough connections between racial and gender discrimination on one hand, and the moral and economic dilemmas that society faced on the other. Gary Dorrien commented that Rauschenbusch and other Social Gospelers "had too little acquaintance with blacks and too little knowledge of African American history to bring racial justice into the purview of social Christianity."[13] Dorrien's comments are instructive with regard to many Social Gospelers, attitudes toward women as well. Rauschenbusch's summons to "Christianize the social order" soon sounded outdated.

Although Scudder greatly appreciated Rauschenbusch's ideas and incorporated many of them into her own social theory, her practical experience provided her with a different perspective. She intentionally aligned herself with groups that would broaden her understanding of the complexity of social problems. Her socialist critique of the society disclosed racial and gender discrimination within an unjust economic system. Her settlement experience, commitment to the Anglican Church and to socialism, friendships with women, and teaching experience—all these broadened her understanding of the systemic problems that society faced. An undercurrent of realism was evident in her work. As Dorrien put it, "She kept her moral idealism on a leash."[14] To state it in another way, Scudder did not share all the faults charged against some other Social Gospel leaders.

The Corporate Church as an Instrument of Redemption

Reinhold Niebuhr was among the next generation of theologians who questioned Social Gospel optimism. Niebuhr witnessed the reformers' dreams for a society free from greed and selfishness dissolve into disillusionment and tarnished optimism. Hit with that reality, Niebuhr thought that moderns had misunderstood human nature by discounting the pervasiveness of sin. Reformers hoped for and attributed too much to their own accomplishments. Scudder agreed with Niebuhr that human beings tended toward arrogance and should feel called to live humble lives. She shared his disappointment when reform movements that had been announced with enthusiasm and powered by human creativity failed to reach the lofty goals their leaders set for them. Scudder, however, also thought Niebuhr failed to understand the impact the corporate Church could make upon its members. The Church had tremendous potential and a special commission to prepare inwardly its members to live as instruments of social redemption, even within a diseased and inhibiting social environment.

Niebuhr's primary complaint was that liberal Christians had mistakenly viewed sin as a moral weakness that could be overcome:

> In liberal Christianity there is an implicit assumption that human nature has the resources to fulfill what the gospel demands. The Kantian axiom, "I ought, therefore I can," is accepted as basic to all analyses of the moral situation. All human actions are simply on a lower or higher scale of rational adjustment to interest and life to life.[15]

Niebuhr argued that human nature was full of sinful contradictions. What made the human spirit distinct among creatures was the human awareness of both its finitude and its freedom. Human beings were capable of recognizing higher values of purity and love, but the conditions of their finitude rendered them incapable of "incarnating all the higher values."[16] Tension would remain between an awareness of God's pure love and the impulse of egoism; one could never conquer the other.

Rauschenbusch discussed the renunciation of sin in terms of entering into "voluntary obedience to God."[17] Individuals renounced sinful behavior by living within the consciousness of the pervading spiritual life of God, which manifested itself in outward action. Conversion meant turning away from selfishness and turning toward God and humanity. Through that change, God rather than the self became the center of the universe. Breaking away from one's sinful past involved submission to God and submission to the common good. Personal salvation affected the social situation by bringing social institutions under the law of Christ. Rauschenbusch then identified redemption with the gradual progress of society toward God's kingdom:

> Complete salvation, therefore, would consist in an attitude of love in which he would freely co-ordinate his life with the life of his fellows in obedience to the loving impulses of the Spirit of God, thus taking his part in a divine organism of mutual service.[18]

For Niebuhr, history had proved that redemption did not happen in this way. God's love stood outside human resources. Human beings could discern the impact of God's love, but their finiteness prevented them from completely transforming themselves or society into a perfect likeness of it. "In classical Christianity the perfectionism of the gospel stands in a much more difficult relation to the estimate of human resources. The love commandment stands in juxtaposition to the fact of sin."[19] God's redemptive activity revealed and contradicted sinful behavior. Liberals' understanding of redemption challenged the self-centeredness of society but left the egotism of the moralists in its place:

> The liberal part of our culture thought that the Christian idea of the sinfulness of all men was outmoded. In its place it put the idea of a harmless egotism, rendered innocuous either by a prudent self-interest or by a balance of all social forces which would transmute the selfishness of all into a higher social harmony. The vanity of that idea was proved by the ever more dynamic disproportion of power in our society and the ever greater destruction of community in a technical society.[20]

Niebuhr concluded that sin was so intricately woven into the fabric of human beings that no sort of practical plan for social change would enable individuals to separate the threads of evil from the threads of goodness within themselves and society. He agreed that sin affected the social order, but at the root of this recognition was God's call for radical humility. Society could engender better social policies but will never reach perfection. Redemption would come from outside the social order, as exemplified by the Christian gospel in the perpetual dying of the self. Only God had the power to provide an "escape from the flux of temporality."[21]

Scudder and Niebuhr were like-minded in several ways. She too emphasized God's call to radical humility, recognized the inability of human beings and society to reach perfection, and questioned the egotism of moralists who viewed materialism as the basis for a solution to society's problems. However, there were also significant differences between their arguments. For Niebuhr, the contradictions of human existence could not be resolved through human action, but only by divine intervention:

> The contradictions of human existences which prevent power from ever being good enough to belong to the kingdom and which equally prevent pure love from being powerful enough to establish itself in the world, must be

> finally overcome; but they can only be overcome by divine action. No human action, proceeding from these contradictions, is equal to it.[22]

Scudder argued that the gospel invited human beings to enter into God's redemptive activity by patterning their lives in accordance with Jesus' voluntary sacrifices. She held on to the belief that by finding the kingdom of God within, human beings would be empowered to restore themselves and their surroundings to harmony with the universe. In her thought, God intervened through the work of human hands.

Taking a road trodden by the mystics, Scudder believed that God was close enough to the beating hearts of humanity to work within human beings for alleviating corruption. Toward the end of her life, Scudder recorded an experience in which she felt that God provided her with an escape from the "flux of temporality." Thinking that death might be imminent, she felt a frightening sense of closeness to God. She wrote in her journal, "When this last happens, I am so frightened—I am an inexpert swimmer suddenly aware that he is out of his depths—so I struggle back frantically—into the floating seaweed."[23] Scudder heavily emphasized the inner discovery of God's Reality through the spiritual journey. She connected the kingdom of God with a state of God consciousness that required a change in attitude of individuals as well as specific changes in society.

Scudder criticized Niebuhr for failing to emphasize the special duty of the Church to prepare its members inwardly to participate in God's redemption of society:

> How great a service [the Church] can render Christendom is startlingly evident if we consider the defeatist tone of a brilliant book much discussed of late—Reinhold Niebuhr's earnest and very Protestant *Moral Man and Immoral Society* (Scribner's, $2.00). Hopelessness of any corporate action to achieve noble ends is the recurrent theme. Christianity, says the author, can at best only mitigate, never defeat, those selfish forces which in complex interweaving control human destiny. By telling illustration of the capacity for hypocrisy and self-delusion in every group surveyed he drives home his sad conviction: "What is lacking among all moralists . . . is an understanding of the brutal character of *all* human collectives." After inexorable exposure of our moralistic sentimentalities comes the conclusion: "There are constitutional limitations in the genus of religion which will always make it more fruitful in purifying individual life and adding wholesomeness to the more intimate social relations than in the problems of the more complex and political

> relations of modern society." Never once does Niebuhr allude to a corporate church as a possible instrument of social redemption![24]

For Scudder, the Christian community played a crucial and distinctive role in leading society into God's vision for it.

Unlike Niebuhr, Scudder did not think of sin as an innate trait that could not be overcome. The duty of the Christian Church was to prepare its members inwardly to be more conscious of God's presence within human hearts and human history. Discerning this presence was not a remedy for sin but a newfound awareness of redemption beyond human shortcomings. She recognized the danger of doubting the seriousness and pervasiveness of human sin and linked her understanding of sin to an attitude of defiant self-protection, which was a consequence of a diseased social environment. Scudder thought that evil lured its victims through the promise of individual wealth and progress at the expense of the larger community's good. Sin was cutting oneself off from the enjoyment of a full relationship with God and with others. Relationships with God and others afforded human beings real freedom. Until humanity opened itself up to the pursuit of real freedom, they remained imprisoned by material things and unable to embody the kind of moral character that God intended for them.

What remains unclear in Scudder's conception of sin is how the environmental pressures that shape moral character are connected to the nature of humanity itself. The social environment in which human beings live shapes their attitudes and practices. At times it seems that Scudder gives the social order a life of its own, which humans can manipulate toward God's ends or leave out of control. But even if God created human beings to act cooperatively and to live in communion, no one can evade social pressures that shape competitive attitudes and practices. This is evident even in Scudder's understanding of the importance of women's work in the home. In Scudder's mind, however, when she deemphasized sin as an intrinsic aspect of human nature, she avoided defining the conversation about human achievement in competitive terms. God intended human beings to live in communion and to act cooperatively. When they did not do so, they failed to live into their true nature. For Scudder, the central theme of the human journey was not to overcome sinful ways but to open oneself up to true intercourse and fellowship with ultimate reality and with all of humanity.

Like Rauschenbusch, Scudder felt a healthy sense of optimism about the ability of human beings to make significant advances toward God's vision for society. Underlying her attitude was her deep belief in God's ability to redeem society through the work of human hands. This attitude, however, did not necessarily imply that Scudder was entirely unrealistic about humans' abilities to participate in social change or manipulate it. According to Scudder, humans did not create moral forces, but as moral agents they reshaped them. Human beings had the potential to bring the world back into harmony with God. Those who acted as effective moral agents did so out of a deeper sense of purpose and drew upon a power other than their own.

An Undercurrent of Realism

Reinhold Niebuhr raised legitimate concerns about Social Gospel optimism. Scudder shared this optimistic outlook by issuing a call to moderns to renounce their egoism: "It is the meek who inherit the earth, after all; and if we want men to possess their heritage, we must set about making them meek."[25] There was, however, an undercurrent of realism evident in her work that did not fit perfectly with either of the Niebuhrs' views of liberalism.

In *Christ and Culture* H. Richard Niebuhr raised a key issue with Rauschenbusch's theology: How did one distinguish between a deeper sense of moral purpose that echoed from God's intentions on one hand, and actions based on selfish motives on the other? Niebuhr argued that the danger of Social Gospel theology was that Christ became the "Christ of culture, and that man's greatest task is to maintain his best culture. . . . Christ is identified with what men conceive to be their finest ideals, their noblest institutions, and their best philosophy."[26] Scudder spoke directly about her concern that prevailing cultural attitudes not be used to validate God's intentions for human beings and the creation. Although she emphasized a personal encounter with God and the impact of the social environment on the formation of one's character, she made a clear distinction between the way society operated on the basis of self-invested competition on one hand, and God's intentions for it on the other.

Perhaps H. Richard Niebuhr's comments about F. D. Maurice's theology are more relevant in relation to Scudder's argument. Maurice believed that the community for which God created human beings extended beyond temporal boundaries to a community of humanity with God, Christ, and the Holy Spirit. Niebuhr said:

> Universal salvation meant more than the turning of individual selves to their true center. By creation through the Word men are social; they are fathers and brothers and wives and husbands, members of nations, spiritual, voluntary

> participants in political, religious, and economic societies. The full realization of the kingdom of Christ did not, then, mean the substitution of a new universal society for all the separate organizations of men, but rather the participation of all these in the one universal kingdom of which Christ is the head. It meant transformation through humiliation and exaltation: through the humiliation which comes when members of the body willingly accept the fact that they are not the head, and through the exaltation which results from the knowledge that they have been given their own particular, necessary work in service to the head of the body and to all its other members.[27]

Scudder's vision for a society fashioned in God's cooperative image was not validated by acceptable cultural mores but affirmed by the overall sense of well-being and cooperation for individuals and others within a larger context. As she focused her social ethic through the lens of Trinitarian doctrine, Scudder envisioned a society that emulated God's cooperative nature. To achieve a better notion of equality, human beings would subvert selfish desires as they recognized their own social nature, their creation in the image of God; for Scudder, this meant "transformation through humiliation and exaltation."

Scudder was well aware of the fact that society would never reach perfection. The Cooperative Commonwealth that she described was not a vision of a perfect paradise. While her call to create an egalitarian social environment was clear, at times her description of the Cooperative Commonwealth was vague and difficult to visualize. She based it not on a static conception of an ideal society, but on an ever-evolving consciousness of the relationship between the self and a greater community. Her hope in opting for socialist policies was that society would choose to move along in harmony with God's natural rhythm, free itself from the tyranny of economic fear, and separate itself from the god of greed. Socialism would create the conditions that were more likely to guard against self-contempt and self-conceit. Perfection, however, would remain out of reach even for a society choosing socialist policies.

Maintaining a strong grasp on the importance of sacrifice in the Christian story, Scudder recognized that socialism could never eliminate suffering from human experience. In *Socialism and Character*, she put it this way:

> For of course suffering will not be eliminated by socialism, and just as pangs that ravage modern souls would have been strange to a contemporary of Virgil, so new sorrows will torture the sensitive race to be.[28]

Jesus' example showed that suffering was not futile and wasted. Scudder emphasized his willingness to endure pain for the greater good of reconstructing a society molded into the likeness of God's cooperative image. For Scudder, the paradox of the cross stood at the center of history as a symbol of God's defiance of worldly values and divinely inspired creativity. The suffering God was the Christian answer to rebellious human agony.

Bernard Markwell suggested that Scudder dealt with the failures of social reforms because her theological perspective "encompassed catastrophe and defeat."[29] He thought that Scudder ultimately abandoned Social Gospel optimism, and he recognized a sense of "realism" in her thought not accounted for in the thought of some other Social Gospelers. When other reformers succumbed to cynicism and regret, Scudder found hope in her theology of the cross. From the lives of the saints, Scudder learned that God did not require her to create the new earth. Her desire for the earth's transformation was enough.

Markwell rightly detected a sense of "realism" in Scudder's theology, but we should not too closely identify Scudder's realism with that of the next generation of theologians. Scudder's realism is more similar to that of Rauschenbusch than to Reinhold Niebuhr's realism. Rauschenbusch wrote:

> In asking for faith in the possibility of a new social order, we ask for no Utopian delusion. . . . We shall never have a perfect social life, yet we must seek it with faith. We shall never abolish suffering. There will always be death and the empty chair and heart. . . . At best there is always but an approximation to a perfect social order. The kingdom of God is always but coming. . . . But every approximation of it is worthwhile.[30]

Rauschenbusch's optimism waned by the time he wrote *A Theology for the Social Gospel*. He still believed in the Social Gospel, but he recognized that social change was complex and would not be inevitable. Commenting on the spiritual unity of his contemporaries, Rauschenbusch alluded to the difficulties that reformers faced:

> If in the most restricted sphere of life we act on the same sinful principles of greed and tyranny on which the great exploiters and despots act, we share their guilt. If we consent to the working principles of the Kingdom of Evil, and do not counteract it with all our strength, but perhaps even fail to see its ruinous evil, then we are part of it and the salvation of Christ has not yet set us free.[31]

Conversion to a new way of cooperative living called for more than just individual breaks with the sinful past. It required separation from the sinful history of a social group. Advancement beyond the "Kingdom of Evil" demanded that all human beings act in ways that were compatible with a consciousness of God. Using Friedrich Schleiermacher's words, Rauschenbusch expressed his awareness that real social solidarity would not be realized until the "totality of all contemporary life"[32] joined together to combat the conditions of sin.

Scudder never thought that any program for social reform would provide an indefinite solution to social ailments. As social circumstances changed, new mechanisms for coping would need to evolve as well. Loyalties to unchanging social ideals caused stagnation; they were "mistaken loyalties to causes of extinguished glory (that) trail their mournful light across the pages of history, as the rays of dead stars wander forever through space."[33] Moral forces were not static but related to the economic necessities of their respective periods. However, the reality that Christians could not attain social perfection did not prevent them from hoping for it. One could not judge the success of reform programs by popularity but rather by the intentions of those devoting themselves to the cause.[34]

Concluding Comments

Vida Dutton Scudder's voice emerged as a distinctive point of view among Social Gospelers. She thought Christian doctrine was flexible enough to address issues that confronted her society, and she interpreted Trinitarian doctrine in light of contemporary social concerns. With the Trinity at the center of her theological ethic, Scudder viewed Divine Society as the model for real democracy and the model for the kind of cooperative behavior that advanced God's kingdom on earth. This theological vision fueled Scudder's social ethic and enabled her to envision possibilities for an egalitarian and cooperative social order.

Believing that the Christian Church was society's best hope to address social problems, Scudder committed herself to working from within the Anglican Communion to address social needs. She acknowledged that the Church often reflected social inequalities but recognized that it had also been gifted with a prophetic voice to speak out against injustices. Christ's suffering and sacrifice modeled for individuals and the community the risk required to bring society back into harmony with God.

Scudder drew upon a rich store of experiences in working with other women and men toward practical reform, teaching within the context of women's colleges, her knowledge of the Christian tradition, and interest in cutting-edge social theory. Influenced by socialism, she connected the class divisions to issues related to gender and race. Through her settlement experience, she sought to break down class barriers that divided her from the working class. Her relationships with women and innovative teaching informed her theories. Scudder's view of the "new woman" sought to increase women's sphere of influence beyond the home. She tried to persuade women to act as the movers and shakers in a new world order. In addition, she nurtured lasting friendships with other more widely remembered leaders such as Walter Rauschenbusch. I am not necessarily convinced that her male contemporaries would have considered her their intellectual equal in the same way that they would a male colleague; nevertheless, the considerable evidence that I have gathered proves that they sought her counsel and support. She entered into the sphere of her male counterparts' influence, and she allowed herself to be influenced by them as well as exercise her influence upon them. She equally shared their sense of prophetic urgency and played a vital role in shaping conversations concerning matters of great theological and ethical importance.

Scudder helped to shape conversations concerning the most pertinent theological and ethical issues of her day. Indeed, she was a significant and creative theological ethicist. Her writings continue to maintain relevance for contemporary conversations as they increase our understanding of the theology that energized the Social Gospel movement and the history of women's involvement in it. Vida Dutton Scudder was no mere onlooker in the movement for reform; as a woman, an activist, and a devout Anglican, she brought a distinctive perspective to bear on the Social Gospel project.

Notes

1. Journal entry, March 14, 1932, Journal 1932–1942. Scudder Papers, Sophia Smith Collection, Smith College Library, Smith College, Northampton, MA.
2. Tribute to Scudder by W. A. Nielson. Scudder Papers, Sophia Smith Collection, Smith College Library, Smith College, Northampton, MA.
3. Author Unknown, *The Living Church* (October 31, 1954). Clipping found in Scudder Files, Archives of the Society of Companions of the Holy Cross, Adelynrood, South Byfield, MA.
4. Author Unknown, *Union City (Indiana) Gazette* (October 13, 1937). Clipping found in Scudder Papers, Wellesley College Archives, Margaret Clapp Library, Wellesley College, Wellesley, MA.
5. Fragment of a newspaper clipping found in Scudder Papers, Wellesley College Archives, Margaret Clapp Library, Wellesley College, Wellesley, MA.

6. Author unknown, *New Haven Register* (April 18, 1937). Clipping found in Scudder Papers, Wellesley College Archives, Margaret Clapp Library, Wellesley College, Wellesley, MA.

7. See Elisabeth Hudnut Clarkson, "Spiritual Tensions in the Early Days of the S.C.H.C.," unpublished, presented as the Opening Paper for the Companions of the Holy Cross Conference of 1994.

8. Sister Mary Theodora, "Wellesley Bookshelf." Fragment of clipping found in Scudder Papers, Wellesley College Archives, Margaret Clapp Library, Wellesley College, Wellesley, MA.

9. "Denison House," *Directory of Clubs and Classes* (1903): 2. College Settlements Papers, Sophia Smith Collection, Smith College Library, Northampton, MA.

10. Randolph Ray to Vida Dutton Scudder, August 16, 1924. Scudder Files, Archives of the Society of Companions of the Holy Cross, Adelynrood, South Byfield, MA.

11. Vida Dutton Scudder, *Education for the New Day* ("Education for the New Day," *The World Tomorrow* 3 [December 1920]: 355–58; repr., New York: Fellowship of Reconciliation, n.d.), 10.

12. Vida Dutton Scudder, "A Pedagogic Sunset," *The Atlantic Monthly* 141 (June 1928): 781.

13. Gary Dorrien, *The Making of American Liberal Theology* (Louisville: Westminster/John Knox Press, 2003), 146.

14. Ibid.

15. Reinhold Niebuhr, *An Interpretation of Christian Ethics* (New York: Harper & Bros., 1937), 65.

16. Ibid., 66.

17. Walter Rauschenbusch, *A Theology for the Social Gospel* (1917; repr., Louisville: Westminster/John Knox Press, 1997), 95.

18. Ibid., 98.

19. Reinhold Niebuhr, *An Interpretation of Christian Ethics*, 65.

20. Reinhold Niebuhr, "The Christian Witness in the Social and National Order," in *Christian Realism and Political Problems* (New York: Charles Scribner's Sons, 1953), 106.

21. Reinhold Niebuhr, *An Interpretation of Christian Ethics*, 69.

22. Reinhold Niebuhr, *Beyond Tragedy: Essays on the Christian Interpretation of History* (New York: Charles Scribner's Sons, 1937), 178.

23. Journal entry, August 28, 1932, Journal of 1932–1933. Scudder Papers, Sophia Smith Collection, Smith College Library, Smith College, Northampton, MA.

24. Vida Dutton Scudder, "The Anglo-Catholic Movement the Next Century: Its Social Outlook," *The Living Church* 90 (March 10, 1934): 589.

25. Scudder, *Education for the New Day*, 6.

26. H. Richard Niebuhr, *Christ and Culture* (New York: Harper & Row, 1951), 102–3.

27. Ibid., 226.

28. Vida Dutton Scudder, *Socialism and Character* (Boston: Houghton, Mifflin, 1912), 250.

29. Bernard K. Markwell, *The Anglican Left* (Brooklyn, NY: Carlson, 1991), 194.

30. Walter Rauschenbusch, *Christianity and the Social Crisis* (1907; repr., Louisville: Westminster/John Knox Press, 1991), 420–21.

31. Rauschenbusch, *A Theology for the Social Gospel*, 92.

32. Ibid., 93.

33. Vida Dutton Scudder, *Socialism and Sacrifice* ("Socialism and Sacrifice," *The Atlantic Monthly* 105 [June 1910]: 836–49; repr., New York: Socialistic Literature Co., n.d.), 14.

34. Scudder, "A Pedagogic Sunset," 781.

Bibliography

Unpublished Works from Archives and Special Collections

Scudder Files. Archives of the Society of Companions of the Holy Cross. Adelynrood. South Byfield, MA.

Scudder Papers. Sophia Smith Collection. Smith College Library. Smith College. Northampton, MA.

Scudder Papers. Wellesley College Archives. Margaret Clapp Library. Wellesley College. Wellesley, MA.

Walter Rauschenbusch Papers. American Baptist Historical Society Manuscript Collection. Samuel Colgate Historical Library. Colgate Rochester Divinity School. Rochester, NY.

Publications by Vida Dutton Scudder

"Pere Antoine." *The Atlantic Monthly* 52 (October 1883): 498–503. (Published under the pseudonym of Davida Coit.)

"Immortality and Evolution." *The New Englander* 7 (September 1884): 707–17.

"Lake of the Poets." *Outlook* 51 (January 19, 1885): 96–97.

"The Poetic Element of Medieval Drama." *The Atlantic Monthly* 56 (September 1885): 407–15. (Published under the pseudonym of Davida Coit.)

"Work for Women at Oxford." *The Christian Union* 33 (April 29, 1886): 7–8; (May 6, 1886): 9–10.

"The Moral Dangers of Musical Devotees." *The Andover Review* 7 (January 1887): 46–53.

"The Effect on Character of College Education: I." *The Christian Union* 35 (April 7, 1887): 12. "II." *The Christian Union* 35 (April 14, 1887): 12. "The Educated Woman as a Social Factor: III." *The Christian Union* 35 (April 21, 1887): 12–13.

"A Protest." *The Christian Union* 35, no. 24 (June 16, 1887): 16.

"The Effect of the Scientific Temper on Modern Poetry." *The Andover Review* 8 (September 1887): 225–46.

"The Effect of the Scientific Temper on Modern Poetry (Concluded)." *The Andover Review* 8 (October 1887): 351–66.

"A Shadow of Gold." *The Overland Monthly* (October 1887): 380–89.

Mitsu-Yu Nissi or The Japanese Wedding. By V. D. S. and Frona M. Brooks. Young's Standard Series of Plays. Boston: H. A. Young & Co., 1888.

"A New Departure in Philanthropy." *The Christian Union* 37 (May 10, 1888): 620–21.

"The Poetry of Matthew Arnold." *The Andover Review* 10 (September 1888): 232–49.

"A Flight in the Dark." By Sophia Kirk (S. K.) and V. D. S. *The Atlantic Monthly* 62 (December 1888): 766–77.

"The Curate's Afterthought." *The Christian Union* 39 (January 17, 1889): 74–75; (January 24, 1889): 106–7.

"Womanhood in Modern Poetry." *Poet Lore* 1 (October 15, 1889): 449–645.

Introduction to the Writings of John Ruskin. The Students' Series of English Classics. Boston: Leach, Shewell, & Sanborn, 1890.

"Influence and Independence." By S. K. and V. D. S. *The Andover Review* 13 (February 1890): 167–81.

"The College Settlements in NYC." *The Dawn* 2 (October 1890): 230–33.

The Relation of College Women to Social Need. Association of Collegiate Alumnae Publications, series 2, no. 3, n.p., 1890.

"A Modern Legend." *Harper's Magazine* 82 (January 1891): 300–303.

"A Comparative Study of Wordsworth's 'Michael,' Tennyson's 'Enoch Arden,' Browning's 'Andrea del Sarto.'" *Poet Lore* 3 (February 16, 1891): 87–93.

"Socialism and Spiritual Progress—A Speculation." An address delivered before the Society of Christian Socialists, Boston, March 1891.

"Wulfy: A Waif: A Christmas Sketch from Life." *The Century* 43 (December 1891): 276–80.

"The Place of College Settlements." *The Andover Review* 18 (October 1892): 339–50.

"A Glimpse into Life." *The Wellesley Magazine* 1 (February 18, 1893): 339–50.

"College Settlements." *The Holy Cross Magazine* 5 (January 1894): 37–38.

The Witness of Denial. New York: Dutton, 1895.

"Two Italian Poets." *The Wellesley Magazine* 3 (January 12, 1895): 185–88.

"College Settlements and Religion." *The Congregationalist* 80 (May 2, 1895): 682.

"Denison House." First in a series of papers by the Society of Companions of the Holy Cross, June 1895.

"Alfred de Vigny." *The Wellesley Magazine* 4 (May 16, 1896): 421–28.

"Notes from Denison House." *Smith College Monthly* 3, no. 6 (March 1896): 42–43.

Life of the Spirit in Modern English Poets. Boston: Houghton, Mifflin, 1897.

"The Greek Spirit in Shelley and Browning." Pages 438–70 in *Papers Selected to Represent the Work of the Society from 1886–1897.* By Boston Browning Society. New York: Macmillan, 1897.

Social Ideals in English Letters. Boston: Houghton, Mifflin, 1898.

Christian Simplicity. The Christian Social Union Publication 52, August 15, 1898. Boston, Office of the Secretary, 1 Joy St., 1898. A rewriting of the 1896 SCHC Paper of the same title.

"Arnold as an Abiding Force." *The Dial* 27 (December 16, 1899): 481–82.

"The College Woman and Social Reform." *Celebration of the Quarter-Centenary of Smith College, October Second and Third, 1900.* Cambridge: Riverside Press, 1900.

"Recollections of Ruskin." *The Atlantic Monthly* 85 (April 1900): 568–71.

"The College Settlements Movement." *Smith College Monthly* 7 (May 1900): 447–54.

"Ill-Gotten Gifts to Colleges." *The Atlantic Monthly* 86 (November 1900): 675–79.

Introduction to the Study of English Literature. New York: Globe School Book Co., 1901.

"The Uses of Poetry." Pages 1–10 in *A Glad New Year.* Department of English Literature, Wellesley College, 1902.

"The Mosaics at Ravenna." *The Churchman* 85 (April 12, 1902): 462–65.

"College Settlements and College Women." *Outlook* 70 (April 19, 1902): 973–76.

"A Hidden Weakness in Our Democracy." *The Atlantic Monthly* 89 (May 1902): 638–44.
"Democracy and Education." *The Atlantic Monthly* 89 (June 1902): 816–22.
"The Shrine of the Narcissus." *The Churchman* 86 (August 23, 1902): 220–21.
"Democracy and Society." *The Atlantic Monthly* 90 (September 1902): 348–52.
"Democracy and the Church." *The Atlantic Monthly* 90 (October 1902): 521–27.
"The Educational Element in Dante's Divine Comedy, I." *The Kindergarten Review* 13 (November 1902): 127–35. "II." *The Kindergarten Review* 13 (December 1902).
A Listener in Babel. Boston: Houghton, Mifflin, 1903.
"Sicilian Holy Days." *The Churchman* 87 (April 11, 1903): 485–88, 491.
"Footprints of St. Francis." *The Outlook* 74 (June 6, 1903): 332–38.
"The Heart of the Alps." *The Churchman* 88 (October 3, 1903): 391–95.
"Modern Innocents Abroad." *Smith College Monthly* 11 (November 1903): 112–24.
Saint Catherine of Siena, as Seen in Her Letters. New York: Houghton, Mifflin, 1905.
"Wayfaring Memories." Pages 135–62 in *Persephone and Other Poems by the Members of the English Literature Department, Wellesley College*. Boston: Fort Hill, 1905.
"The Irish Literary Drama." *Poet Lore* 16 (March 1905): 40–53.
"Denison House and the Italians." *Chicago Commons* 10 (May 1905): 287–90.
The Disciple of a Saint: Being the Imaginary Biography of Raniero di Landoccio de Pagliaresi. New York: Dutton; London: Dent, 1907.
"The Social Conscience of the Future: I." *The Hibbert Journal* 7 (January 1909): 314–22. "II." *The Hibbert Journal* 7 (April 1909): 578–95.
"Ten Years Later." *The Jabberwock*, February 1909. Magazine of the Girls' Latin School, Boston. Clipping in Scudder papers, Wellesley College Archives.
"Experiment in Fellowship." *The Survey* 22 (April 3, 1909): 47–51.
"The Social Conscience of the Future." *The Hibbert Journal* 7 (October 1909): 190–92.
The Ecclesiastical History of the English Nation. Everyman's Library. London: Dent, 1910.

The Journal and Other Writings of John Woolman. Everyman's Library. London: Dent, 1910.

"Christianity in the Socialist State." *The Hibbert Journal* 8 (April 1910): 562–81.

"Religion and Socialism." *Harvard Theological Review* 3 (April 1910): 230–47.

"Socialism and Sacrifice." *The Atlantic Monthly* 105 (June 1910): 836–49.

"Cathedral Tower." *Chautauqua* 61 (December 1910): 86–87.

"Socialism as the Basis of Religious Unity." In *The Unity of Life: Proceedings and Papers of the National Federation of Religious Liberals Held in New York, April 26–28, 1911*. Edited by Henry W. Wilbur. Philadelphia: The Federation, 1911.

"Class Consciousness." *The Atlantic Monthly* 107 (March 1911): 320–30.

"Forerunners." *The Atlantic Monthly* 107 (August 1911): 231–42.

Socialism and Character. London: J.M. Dent and Sons, Ltd., 1912.

"A Settlement Opportunity." *The Wellesley College News* 20, no. 18 (February 15, 1912): 1.

"Miss Scudder's Criticized Speech: Just What She Said at a Citizens' Meeting in Lawrence, to Which Exception Has Been So Excitedly Taken by the Brahmins." *The Boston Common*, March 9, 1912, 6–7. Repr. in *The Outlook* 100 (April 20, 1912): 846–47.

"Aliens' Fine Qualities." Letter to the Editor. *Boston Globe*, March 17, 1912.

"For Justice' Sake." *The Survey* 28 (April 16, 1912): 76–79.

"On Magic Casements." *The Century Magazine* 85 (December 1912): 316–18.

"The Moral Assets of the Class Struggle: Address of Miss Vida D. Scudder at the Ford Hall Meeting, January 12, 1913." *Ford Hall Folks* 1, no. 4 (January 19, 1913): 2–6.

"More Abundant Life." *Life and Labor* 3, no. 3 (March 1913): 1.

"An Awakening in New England." *Everyman* 24 (March 28, 1913): 742.

"Why Doesn't the Church Turn Socialist?" *The Coming Nation* (NS) 133 (March 29, 1913): 9–10.

"Why Join the Party?" *The Intercollegiate Socialist* 2 (October–November 1913): 5–7.

"Masefield and Gibson: A Renaissance in Social Poetry." *The Survey* 31 (March 7, 1914): 707–9.

"The Church's Great Opportunity." *The Churchman* 109 (April 4, 1914): 434–36.

"Woman and Socialism." *The Yale Review* 3 (April 1914): 454–70.
"The Passing of College Hall, Wellesley." *The Churchman* 109 (April 14, 1914): 434–36.
"The Church Socialist League." *The Churchman* 110 (August 8, 1914): 183–84.
"Women and the Present Crisis." *The Social Preparation for the Kingdom of God* (November 1914): 76–77.
"Some Signs of Hope." *The Intercollegiate Socialist* 3 (April–May 1915): 6–8.
"Religious Life." *The Wellesley College News* 23 (April 1915): 39–40.
"Plato as a Novelist." *The Yale Review* (NS) 4 (July 1915): 788–804.
Letter to the Editor. *The Masses* 8, no. 2 (December 1915): 21. Repr. in *The Church and the Hour*. New York: Dutton, 1917.
"The Ethics of Socialism." Address given at Labor Day Weekend Conference by V. D. S.
"The Alleged Failure of the Church to Meet the Social Emergency." Pages 133–53 in *Papers and Addressees of the Thirty-third Church Congress (of the Protestant Episcopal Church) in the United States: Norfolk, VA. May 2–5, 1916*. New York: Edwin S. Gorham, 1916.
Letter to the editor. *The Masses* 8, no. 4 (February 1916): 20. Repr. in *The Church and the Hour*. New York: Dutton, 1917.
"Academic Freedom." *The Century Magazine* 92 (June 1916): 222–30.
"Remarks of Chairman of Session of Intercollegiate Socialist Society Annual Convention, December, 1916." As quoted by Harry Laidler in "Jottings from the I.S.S. Convention." *The Intercollegiate Socialist* 5 (February–March 1917): 14–15.
The Church and the Hour. New York: Dutton, 1917.
"The Alleged Failure of the Church." *The Yale Review* 6 (January 1917): 327–28.
"A Plea for Social Intercession." *The Churchman* 115 (January 6, 1917): 9–10.
"Strength, Song, Salvation." *The Churchman* 115 (March 17, 1917).
"Socialists and the Problem of War: A Symposium." *The Intercollegiate Socialist* 5 (April–May 1917): 7, 20–21.
"The Doubting Pacifist." *The Yale Review* 6 (July 1917): 738–51.
Editorial. *The Social Preparation for the Kingdom of God* 4 (October 1917): 12–14.
"A Christmas Message." *The Churchman* 116 (December 22, 1917): 804–5.
"A Pacifist in War Time." Clipping in Scudder Papers at Wellesley, n.d.

"Bishop Jones and Reaction on the Church." Letter to the editor. *The Churchman* 117 (January 12, 1918): 65.
"What of the Church?—A Discussion." *The New World* 1 (April 1918): 79–81.
Editorial. *The Social Preparation for the Kingdom of God* 5 (July 1918): 12–13.
"How Draw Workingmen to Church?" *The American Church Monthly* 4 (September 1918): 26–35.
A Church Year-Book of Social Justice. New York: Dutton, 1919.
"Prophecy Coming True." *The Social Preparation for the Kingdom of God* 5 (January 1919): 12–14.
"Pacifism—Prof. Scudder's Denial of This Title." *Boston Globe* (January 26, 1919).
"The Church and the League of Nations." *The World Tomorrow* 2 (February 1919): 54.
"The Social Teachings of the Church Year." *Anglican Theological Review* 1 (March 1919): 383–406.
"The Strike in Lawrence." *The Christian Register* 98, no. 18 (May 1919): 416–18.
"The Church Today." *Anglican Theological Review* 2 (October 1919): 106–13.
"Seed-Vessel Time." *The Atlantic Monthly* 124 (November 1919): 717–20. Repr. in *The Privilege of Age*. New York: Dutton, 1939.
"Beyond Stewardship." *The Living Church* 62, no. 3 (November 15, 1919): 77–78.
"Almost Too Good to Be True." *The World Tomorrow* 2 (December 1919): 323–25.
"The Socialist Review." *The Socialist Review* 8 (December 1919): 48–49.
"John Woolman Today." *The Friend* 93 (March 1920): 434–37.
"On Being a Stockholder." *The New Republic* 23 (July 14, 1920): 198–200.
"The New Chivalry." *The Venturer* (October 1920): 31–36.
"Education for the New Day." *The World Tomorrow* 3 (December 1920): 355–58.
Social Teachings of the Christian Year. New York: Dutton, 1921.
"Is the Christian Church Christian? From Another Point of View." *The Christian Century* 38 (April 7, 1921): 11–14.
"What Is Luxury?" *The World Tomorrow* 5 (June 1922): 163–64. Repr. in *The Privilege of Age*. New York: Dutton, 1939.
"Fear Not." *The Social Preparation for the Kingdom of God* 9 (July/October, 1922): 8–9.

"Property and Creative Joy." *The Christian Century* 41 (November 9, 1922): 1392–94.
"The Last Beatitude." *The Witness* 7 (February 1923): 7–8.
"Franciscan Parallels." *Anglican Theological Review* 5 (March 1923): 282–98.
"The Church League for Industrial Democracy." *The Church Militant* (March 1923): 9.
"Christian Motives and Economic Reform." *The Congregationalist* 108, no. 27 (July 5, 1923): 8–9.
"Christianity: Conservative or Revolutionary?" *The World Tomorrow* 7 (August 1924): 244–45.
"The College Girl's Mind." *The New Republic* 40 (October 1, 1924): 123–24. Repr. in *The Privilege of Age*. New York: Dutton, 1939.
"Christianity in the Next Fifty Years." *The Western Christian Advocate* (January 15, 1925).
"Forerunners of the C.L.I.D.: Our Heritage from the Past." *The Witness* 9 (September 24, 1925).
"Why the Saints?" *The Commonweal* 3 (December 9, 1925): 127–29.
"A Modern Saint of the Fourteenth Century: A Non-Catholic Appreciation of St. Catherine." *Rosary Magazine* 48 (April 1926): 1–6.
Brother John: A Tale of the First Franciscans. Boston: Little, Brown, 1927.
"The Bishops' Crusade to Stir Our Wills to Action." *The Witness* 11, no. 22 (January 20, 1927): 41–44.
"The Social Conscience of American Churches." *The Commonwealth* (London) 32 (February 1927): 41–44.
"Sons of Francis: What Is Their Legacy?" *The Churchman* 125, no. 10 (March 5, 1927): 16–17.
"Brother John: Monk and Friar." *The Churchman* 125, no. 14 (April 2, 1927): 12–14.
"Forever Arriving." A contribution to the symposium "Why Utopias Never Come." *The Adult Bible Class Magazine* (June 1927): 258–59.
"The Privileges of a College Teacher." *The Wellesley Alumnae Magazine* 11 (August 1927): 327–29.
"A Pedagogic Sunset." *The Atlantic Monthly* 141 (June 1928): 781–91.
"The Franciscan Studies Summer School at Oxford." *The Tablet* (August 18, 1928): 215–17.
"The Larks of St. Francis." *The World Tomorrow* 11 (December 1928): 503–4.
"The Federal Council of Churches: A Report." *The Witness* 13, no. 19 (December 27, 1928): 3–4.

"A Wandering Mind in Italy." *Wellesley College Literary Review* (January 1929): 3–7.
"Mysticism and Social Passion." *The World Tomorrow* 13 (March 1930): 122–25.
"Adventuring for God." *The Congregationalist* 115 (April 24, 1930): 549, 558.
"The Social Duty of Catholics." *The American Church Monthly* 27 (May 1930): 335–42.
"The Franciscan Adventure." *The Atlantic Monthly* 145 (June 1930): 808–19.
Franciscan Adventure. Toronto: Dent, 1931.
"Can the Church Be Saved?" *The Christian Century* 48 (January 21, 1931): 82–85.
"The Waiting Task." *Christendom* (London) 1 (June 1931): 121–28.
"The Church and Industry." *The Witness* 16 (September 24, 1931): 8–9.
"Thanksgiving and Hard Times: If You Were President, How Would You Proclaim Thanksgiving Day?" *The Christian Century* 48 (November 18, 1931): 1457.
"The Christian Way Out." *The Witness* 16, no. 27 (February 25, 1932): 4–5.
"Christian and Churchwoman: Why?" *The Living Church* 87 (August 13, 1932): 355.
"St. Francis and Today." *The CSS Review* (Christ Seva Sangha Ashram, Poona, India) 2 (October 1932): 279–83.
"The Privilege of Age." *The Atlantic Monthly* 151 (February 1933): 205–11. Repr. in *The Privilege of Age*. New York: Dutton, 1939.
"A Franciscan Episode." *The Churchman* 147, no. 19 (August 15, 1933): 16–17.
"The Next Hundred Years of the Catholic Revival: II. Alternatives and Opportunities." *Christendom* (London) 3 (September 1933): 190–99. Repr. in *The Privilege of Age*. New York: Dutton, 1939.
"A Franciscan Institute." *The Commonweal* 18 (September 1, 1933): 427–28.
"The Cross in Utopia." *The Hibbert Journal* 32 (October 1933): 56–69.
The Christian Attitude toward Private Property. New Tracts for New Times. Milwaukee: Morehouse Publishing Co., 1934. Repr. in *The Privilege of Age*. New York: Dutton, 1939.
Christian Citizenship: Presented at the Triennial Meeting of the Woman's Auxiliary of the National Council, Atlantic City, New Jersey. New York: Women's Auxiliary, 1934.
"Social Problems Facing the Church in 1934." *The Spirit of Missions* 99 (January 1934): 6–9. Repr. as *The Church and Social Justice*. New York: The National Council, Department of Christian Social Service, 1934.

"Christian Conflicts." *Christendom* (London) 4, no. 3 (March 1934): 12–23.

"The Anglo-Catholic Movement in the Next Century: Its Social Outlook." *The Living Church* 90 (March 10, 1934): 589–91.

"St. Catherine of Siena." *The Holy Cross Magazine* (April 1934): 147–50.

"St. Bonaventure." *The Holy Cross Magazine* (July 1934): 147–50.

"A Conference of the Eastern Church." *The Living Church* 91 (August 11, 1934): 213.

"St. Francis of Assisi." *The Holy Cross Magazine* (October 1934): 219–34.

"Promise and Problem." *The Living Church* 91 (November 17, 1934): 619–20.

"Work." *The Hibbert Journal* 33 (July 1935): 498–510. Repr. in *The Privilege of Age*. New York: Dutton, 1939.

On Journey. New York: Dutton, 1937.

"Varieties of the Christian Experience." *The Holy Cross Magazine* (January 1937): 17–19.

"A Little Tour in the Mind of Lenin." *The Christian Century* 54 (March 24, 1937): 379–82. Repr. in *The Privilege of Age*. New York: Dutton, 1939.

"The Art of Corporate Worship." A review of *Worship*, by Evelyn Underhill. *Christendom* (Chicago) 2 (Summer 1937): 376–87. Repr. in *The Privilege of Age*. New York: Dutton, 1939.

"C.L.I.D. at General Convention." Letter to the editor. *The Living Church* 97 (September 25, 1937): 358–59.

"Now! Now!" *The Living Church* 98 (January 19, 1938): 73–74.

". . . The Price of Liberty." *The Commonweal* 27 (April 15, 1938): 680–82.

"Prophetic Elements in the Franciscan Movement." *Christendom* (Chicago) 3 (Summer 1938): 378–90.

"Conflicting Loyalties." *Radical Religion* 3 (Winter 1938): 9–12.

The Privilege of Age: Essays Secular and Spiritual. New York: Dutton, 1939.

"The United Front." *The Living Church* 100 (January 4, 1939): 15–16.

"The Discipline of Wartime." *Unity* (November 6, 1939).

Father Huntington: Founder of the Order of the Holy Cross. New York: Dutton, 1940.

"The Cross Eternal: I." *Holy Cross Magazine* (September 1940): 226–29. "II." *Holy Cross Magazine* (October 1940): 296–99.

"Father Huntington." *The Living Church* 102, no. 4 (December 18, 1940): 2.

"The Significance of Malvern for American Churchmen." *The Living Church* 103, no. 8 (March 5, 1941): 13–14.

"Consummation." *The Witness* 25, no. 3 (March 27, 1941): 3–4.
"Footnote on Father Huntington." *The Living Church* 103, no. 11 (April 2, 1941): 11.
"The War and God's Judgment." *The Living Church* 103, no. 11 (April 2, 1941): 10–11.
"Foemen Vassals: A Pacifist Apologia." *The Protestant* 4, no. 2 (October–November 1941): 45–54.
"Messages from Malvern." *The Witness* 25 (November 6, 1941): 7–9.
"Denison House: A Community Center for Real Democracy." *Denison House Herald* 8, no. 5 (December 1941): 1
"Know Your Classics." *The Witness* 25, no. 34 (December 4, 1941): 3.
"The Confessions of St. Augustine." *The Witness* 25, no. 38 (January 8, 1942): 9.
"The Rule of St. Benedict." *The Witness* 25, no. 42 (February 5, 1942): 10.
"The Dream of the Rood." *The Witness* 25, no. 46 (March 5, 1942): 9.
"The Book of St. Bernard on the Love of God." *The Witness* 25, no. 49 (March 26, 1942): 10.
"Malvern 1941." *The Living Church* 104, no. 24 (June 14, 1942): 10–11.
"Franciscan Leaven." *The Friend* (Philadelphia) 117 (Eleventh Month 1943): 147–49.
"Foreword." *Letters to Her Companions* by Emily Malbone Morgan. With a biographical sketch by Emily Sophie Brown. The Society of the Companions of the Holy Cross: South Byfield, MA, 1944.
"The Church Holds the Key to Peace." *Forth* (November 1944): 7.
"Jerusalem, Not Geneva." Letter to the editor. *The Christian Century* 62 (January 17, 1945): 82–83.
"John Woolman: Precursor." *The Witness* 28 (April 5, 1945): 8–9.
"The Secret Work of Grace: A Whitsuntide Meditation." *The Holy Cross Magazine* (May 1945): 141–42.
"William Blake: Christian Revolutionist." *The Witness* 28 (May 17, 1945): 7–8.
"Frustration: A Note of Cheer." *Saturday Review of Literature* 28 (November 17, 1945): 60.
"Raphael M. Huber: A Documented History of the Franciscan Order 1182–1517." *Franciscan Studies* 6 (March 1946): 93–99.
"How to Pray in These Difficult Days." *The Church Woman* (June 1946): 5–8.
"Anglican Thought on Property." Pages 124–50 in *Christianity and Property*. Edited by Joseph Fletcher. Philadelphia: Westminster, 1947.

"Social Rebirth: First of a Series on Social Rebirth." *The Witness* 30, no. 37 (October 16, 1947): 11–12. "The Church and Social Rebirth: The Final of a Series," *The Witness* 30 (December 4, 1947): 9–11.
My Quest for Reality. Wellesley, MA: Printed for the author, 1952.

Other Works Consulted

Abell, Aaron Ignatius. *The Urban Impact on American Protestantism, 1865–1900*. Cambridge, MA: Harvard University Press, 1943.
Addams, Jane. *The Social Thought of Jane Addams*. Edited by Christopher Lasch. Indianapolis: Bobbs-Merrill, 1965.
———. *Twenty Years at Hull House*. New York: Macmillan, 1911.
Aptheker, Herbert, ed. *Marxism and Christianity: A Symposium*. New York: Humanities Press, 1968.
Beckley, Harlan. *Passion for Justice*. Louisville: Westminster/John Knox Press, 1992.
Binyon, Gilbert Clive. *The Christian Socialist Movement in England*. New York: Macmillan, 1931.
Block, Walter, and Irving Hexham, eds. *Religion, Economics, and Social Thought*. International Symposium on Religion, Economics, and Social Thought (1982: Vancouver, BC). Vancouver, BC: The Fraser Institute, 1986.
Boonin-Vail, Martha Clara. "New Wine in Old Bottles: Anglo-Catholicism in the United States, 1840–1919." PhD diss., Yale University, 1993.
Corcoran, Teresa. *Vida Dutton Scudder*. Boston: Twayne, 1982.
———. "Vida Dutton Scudder: The Impact of World War I on the Radical Woman Professor." *Anglican Theological Review* 57 (April 1975): 164–81.
———. "Vida Dutton Scudder and the Lawrence Textile Strike of 1912." *Essex Institute Historical Collections* 125 (July 1979): 183–95.
———. "Vida Dutton Scudder: The Progressive Years." PhD diss., Georgetown University, 1973.
Crimmins, James, ed. *Religion, Secularization, and Political Thought*. New York: Routledge, 1990.
Curtis, Susan. *A Consuming Faith: The Social Gospel and Modern American Culture*. Baltimore: Johns Hopkins University Press, 1991.
Davis, Allen F. *Spearheads for Reform: The Social Settlements and the Progressive Movement, 1890–1914*. New York: Oxford University Press, 1967.

Dombrowski, James. *The Early Days of Christian Socialism in America*. New York: Columbia University Press, 1936.

Dorrien, Gary J. *The Making of American Liberal Theology: Idealism, Realism, and Modernity 1900–1950*. Louisville: Westminster/John Knox Press, 2003.

Ely, Richard. *The Social Aspects of Christianity*. New York: Thomas Y. Crowell, 1889.

———. *Socialism and Social Reform*. New York: Thomas Y. Crowell, 1894.

Evans, Christopher. *The Kingdom Is Always But Coming: A Life of Walter Rauschenbusch*. Grand Rapids: Eerdmans, 2004.

———, ed. *The Social Gospel Today*. Louisville: Westminster/John Knox Press, 2001.

Frederick, Peter J. *Knights of the Golden Rule: The Intellectual as Christian Social Reformer in the 1890s*. Lexington: University of Kentucky Press, 1976.

Friedman, Milton. *Capitalism and Freedom*. Chicago: University of Chicago Press, 1962.

Gladden, Washington. *Burning Questions of the Life That Now Is, and of That Which Is to Come*. New York: Century, 1890.

———. *How Much Is Left of the Old Doctrines?* Boston: Houghton, Mifflin, 1899.

Green, Harvey. *The Light of the Home: An Intimate View of the Lives of Women in Victorian America*. New York: Pantheon Books, 1983.

Griffith, Gwilym Oswald. *Mazzini: Prophet of Modern Europe*. London: Hodder & Stoughton, 1932.

Gustafson, James. *Protestant and Roman Catholic Ethics*. Chicago: University of Chicago Press, 1978.

Handlin, Oscar. *Boston's Immigrants, 1790–1880: A Study in Acculturation* (esp. 54–150). New York: Atheneum, 1972.

Handy, Robert. *The Social Gospel in America, 1870–1920*. New York: Oxford University Press, 1966.

Hopkins, Charles. *The Rise of the Social Gospel in American Protestantism, 1865–1915*. New Haven: Yale University Press, 1940.

Kipnis, Ira. *The American Socialist Movement, 1897–1912*. New York: Columbia University Press, 1952.

Lagerquist, L. DeAne. "Woman and the American Religious Pilgrimage: Vida Scudder, Dorothy Day, and Pauli Murray." Pages 208–28 in *New Dimensions in American Religious History*. Edited by Jay P. Nolan and James P. Wind. Grand Rapids: Eerdmans, 1993.

Lindley, Susan. "Neglected Voices and Praxis in the Social Gospel." *Journal of Religious Ethics* (Spring 1990): 75–84.

———. *"You Have Stept Out of Your Place": A History of Women and Religion in America.* Louisville: Westminster/John Knox Press, 1996.

Lindsey, William. "The Social Gospel and Feminism." *American Journal of Theology and Philosophy* 13, no. 3 (September 1992): 195–210.

Lukács, Georg. *History and Class Consciousness: Studies in Marxist Dialectics* (esp. 46–82). Translated by Rodney Livingstone. Cambridge, MA: MIT Press, 1971.

Mann, Arthur. *Yankee Reformers in an Urban Age.* Cambridge, MA: Harvard University Press, 1954.

Markwell, Bernard K. *The Anglican Left.* Brooklyn, NY: Carlson, 1991.

Marx, Karl. *Capital, The Communist Manifesto and Other Writings.* New York: The Modern Library, 1959.

Maurice, Frederick D. *The Life of Frederick Denison Maurice.* Vol. 1. New York: Charles Scribner's Sons, 1884.

———. "Light and Darkness: Sin and Purification." In *Reconstructing Christian Ethics.* Edited by Ellen K. Wondra. Louisville: Westminster/John Knox Press, 1995.

May, Henry F. *Protestant Churches and Industrial America.* New York: Harper & Bros., 1949; repr., New York: Octagon Books, 1963.

Niebuhr, H. Richard. *Christ and Culture.* New York: Harper & Row, 1951.

Niebuhr, Reinhold. *Beyond Tragedy: Essays on the Christian Interpretation of History.* New York: Charles Scribner's Sons, 1937.

———. "The Christian Witness in the Social and National Order." Page 106 in *Christian Realism and Political Problems.* New York: Charles Scribner's Sons, 1953. Repr. Fairfield, NJ: August M. Kelley, 1977.

———. *An Interpretation of Christian Ethics.* New York: Harper & Brothers, 1937.

———. *Love and Justice: Selections from the Shorter Writings of Reinhold Niebuhr.* Edited by D. B. Robertson. Philadelphia: Westminster, 1957.

Norman, Edward R. *Church and Society in England, 1770–1970.* Oxford: Clarendon, 1976.

———. *The Victorian Christian Socialists.* Cambridge: Cambridge University Press, 1987.

Ottati, Douglas F. "Assessing Moral Arguments: A Study." Unpublished Paper (September 1987).

Pacey, Lorene M., ed. *Readings in the Development of Settlement Work.* New York: Association, 1950.

Palmieri, Patricia. *In Adamless Eden*. New Haven: Yale University Press, 1995.

Phillips, Paul T. *A Kingdom on Earth: Anglo-American Social Christianity, 1880–1940*. University Park, PA: The Pennsylvania State University Press, 1996.

Pinn, Anthony B., ed. *Making the Gospel Plain: The Writings of Bishop Reverdy C. Ransom*. Harrisburg: Trinity Press International, 1999.

Rauschenbusch, Walter. *Christianity and the Social Crisis*. 1907. Repr., Louisville: Westminster/John Knox Press, 1991.

———. *Christianizing the Social Order*. New York: Macmillan, 1912.

———. "Is the Woman's Movement Going to Save Society?" *Ford Hall Folks* 2, no. 28 (April 26, 1914).

———. *A Theology for the Social Gospel*. 1917. Repr., Louisville: Westminster/John Knox Press, 1997.

Reckitt, Maurice B. *Faith and Society: A Study of the Structure, Outlook and Opportunity of the Christian Social Movement in Great Britain and the United States of America*. London: Longmans, Green, 1932.

———. *Maurice to Temple: A Century of the Social Movement in the Church of England*. London: Faber & Faber, 1946.

Ricardo, David. *The Principles of Political Economy and Taxation*. 1911. Repr., London: Everyman's Library, 1965.

Ruether, Rosemary Radford, and Rosemary Skinner Keller, eds. *In Our Own Voices*. San Francisco: HarperSanFrancisco, 1995.

Shaw, George Bernard, ed. *The Fabian Essays in Socialism*. 1889. Repr., London: George Allen & Unwin, 1950.

Shepheard, Harold Beaumont. *Jesus and Politics: An Essay towards an Ideal*. New York: Dutton, 1915.

Simkhovitch, Mary. "The Settlement and Religion." Page 142 in *Readings in the Development of Settlement Work*. Edited by Lorene M. Pacey. New York: Association, 1950.

Spencer, Ralph. "Anna Howard Shaw." *Methodist History* 13 (January 1975): 33–51.

Smith, Gary Scott. "Creating a Cooperative Commonwealth: Vida Scudder's Quest to Reconcile Christianity and Socialism, 1890–1920." *Anglican and Episcopal History* 62 (September 1993): 397–428.

Smith, Marilyn Howley. "Vida Dutton Scudder and Social Reform: A Theology of Hope." PhD diss., St. Louis University, 1996.

Stackhouse, Max. L. *Public Theology and Political Economy: Christian Stewardship in Modern Society* (esp. 52–74). Grand Rapids: Eerdmans, 1987.

Visser 'T Hooft, Willem A. *The Background of the Social Gospel in America*. 1928. Repr., St. Louis: Bethany, 1968.

Weinstein, James. *The Decline of Socialism in America, 1912–1925*. New York: Random House, 1967.

White, Ronald C., Jr. *Liberty and Justice for All: Radical Reform and the Social Gospel (1877–1925)*. San Francisco: Harper & Row, 1990.

White, Ronald C., Jr., and Charles Howard Hopkins. *The Social Gospel: Religion and Reform in Changing America*. Philadelphia: Temple University Press, 1976.

Wolf, William J., John E. Booty, and Owen C. Thomas, eds. *The Spirit of Anglicanism: Hooker, Maurice, Temple*. Wilton, CT: Morehouse-Barlow, 1979.

Index